3/24/93

CAMPFOLLOWING

CAMPFOLLOWING

A History of the Military Wife

BETTY SOWERS ALT
AND
BONNIE DOMROSE STONE

New York
Westport, Connecticut
London

Library of Congress Cataloging-in-Publication Data

Alt, Betty Sowers.
    Campfollowing : a history of the military wife / Betty Sowers Alt
and Bonnie Domrose Stone.
      p. cm.
    ISBN 0–275–93721–6 (alk. paper).—ISBN 0–275–93722–4 (pbk. :
alk. paper)
    1. United States—Armed Forces—Military life. 2. Military wives—
United States.   I. Stone, Bonnie Domrose.   II. Title.
III. Title: Campfollowing.
    U766.A45   1991
    355.1′2′0973—dc20   90–24999

British Library Cataloguing in Publication Data is available.

Library of Congress Catalog Card Number: 90–24999
ISBN: 0–275–93721–6 (hb.)
      0–275–93722–4 (pbk.)

First published in 1991

Praeger Publishers, One Madison Avenue, New York, NY   10010
An imprint of Greenwood Publishing Group, Inc.

Printed in the United States of America

∞

The paper used in this book complies with the
Permanent Paper Standard issued by the National
Information Standards Organization (Z39.48–1984).

10 9 8 7 6 5 4 3 2 1

For Leighton and Bill
and for Lem

CONTENTS

INTRODUCTION

You know it takes something special in a woman to live in a situation where she knows time and time again that she and the children are number two.

Maureen Mylander, quoting a
general in *The Generals*

In the cool dampness of a tree-lined military graveyard in a century-old fort in Washington State lie buried men who have served their country well. Interspersed among their graves are remains of some military wives. On the tombstones are engraved only the wives' first names and the ranks of their husbands. In death, so little is known about these women who gave up so much—families and friends—to take up campfollowing for most of their married lives.

These anonymous women are our unsung heroines who for more than 200 years braved wars to tend to their husbands, trekked the great American deserts and plains of the West, crossed the roiling waters of the Pacific, and survived violent political upheavals worldwide. When the great or small wars took their husbands overseas, each followed as far as she could, then set about to keep the home fires burning. Today, more than ever, the military wife is a pioneer who travels to strange lands, rears her family under nomadic and often inhospitable conditions, and, many times copes with the stress of surviving on her own.

It does take a special kind of woman to be a military wife. She must be a patriot, and a helpmate, lover, comforter, and confidant to her husband. As one reads the early diaries or hears the stories of women who have experienced the roller-coaster ups and downs of military life, it becomes clear that a military wife must be courageous and resilient, and have a sense of humor. Her husband and his job will always come first; to be a good military wife, she must cheerfully yield satisfaction of her needs and desires to the needs of the military. It is neither an easy life nor one to which all wives can adapt, but those who do are part of a heritage rich in sacrifice, adventure, and fulfillment.

There are many volumes filled with the exploits of military men, but the heritage and lifestyle of the military wife is relatively unknown. The pages of *Campfollowing* are filled with the lives of these special women, whose two-hundred-year story is told for the first time.

Because published records contain only casual and incomplete information on early military wives, extensive library research was needed to glean evidence of the contributions made by these women as they supported American military men. Unpublished diaries and letters add personal insights into the experiences Army couples shared in the late nineteenth and early twentieth centuries. Interviews with wives from all services, all ranks, and all ages—from those whose husbands served in World War I to those whose spouses are presently on active duty—bring their story to the brink of the twenty-first century.

None of these women had special training for this job. Each was (and still is) the girl next door who married a soldier or whose husband was suddenly a draftee. She would experience pangs of separation and loneliness, excitement at travel and experiencing new cultures, and all too often, grief over the injury to or loss of her spouse. The authors each have the personal insight of over twenty years "campfollowing," which gives added depth to the interviews.

This book is dedicated to all those women—from 1776 to the present—who shared and survived the military adventure with their husbands, and having done so established the rich tradition of campfollowing. To all of you who so freely shared your stories, we are grateful. We are also grateful to Sandra Engle for her faith in and help with our efforts.

CAMPFOLLOWING

CHAPTER ONE

LADIES OF THE REVOLUTION

Bitter December winds howled across the ice-rimmed fields at Valley Forge, freezing the life and vitality of the soldiers of the Continental Army. Young men, many no more than boys, suffered from wounds, disease, and malnutrition. Tents and crude huts were woefully inadequate protection from the subfreezing cold that knifed through the men's tattered clothing, which was per-petually soaked and frozen to their bodies. Feet, scarcely pro-tected with a few rags, turned black with frostbite. Washington's rebel army was at its lowest ebb. Suddenly a shout was heard from the sentries as a cavalcade pushed slowly up the valley through the snow. Bundled against the numbing cold, ten women in carts were bringing to the starving troops "tons of meal and other supplies."[1]

In this devastating winter of 1777, some of the men would be joined at Valley Forge by their wives and families—the first American campfollowers. By accompanying their husbands and sharing their hardships, these women were setting a precedent for the millions of wives who would follow their husbands to forts and encampments worldwide during the more than 200-year history of the American military. These brave women of the Continental Army, estimated to be more than 20,000,[2] dodged bullets, nursed the wounded, foraged for food, cooked, knitted garments for the men, and served as water and ammunition carriers. Beginning the service wives' tradition of placing the needs of the military first, they maintained some semblance of domestic life and became an essential thread in the historical tapestry of the American military system.

Of course, the military in the late 1700s in no way resembled the armed forces of today. Instead of millions of men in uniform, most years the Continental Army consisted of only several thousand. These were chiefly untrained and undisciplined farmers and shopkeepers who were requisitioned on a yearly basis from each of the colonies.[3] When Washington was at Morristown, New Jersey, in May 1777, his force totaled 7,500. In August 1777, when the general marched through Philadelphia

> with drums beating, the flag of the Union (13 stars and stripes) flying, the generals and their aides all gold and lace riding on frisky mounts, and the "ragged, lousy, naked regiments" carrying burnished arms, the whole force came up to the magnificent total of 11,000 fit for duty.[4]

Logistics was a significant problem in the Continental Army. Pay for the soldiers was sporadic at best. The most basic needs of the fighting man—uniforms, transport, food, housing, and ammunition—were often supplied by the troops themselves or their families. Officers, most with personal resources, tended to be better equipped and housed.

The Continental Army was a recent entity in the New World. It had no tradition to imitate other than that of its rival, Great Britain. Consequently, it is not surprising that a pseudo-artistocratic officer class developed which was organizationally and socially separate from the enlisted or "serving class." Although Continental Army officers were often elected by their men, many of the officer ranks were filled by wealthy landowners or merchants[5] whose assets helped ease for them the hardships faced by the common soldier. In this first war, then, were the beginnings of the military aristocracy which would blossom into a full-blown, powerful caste system that remained firmly entrenched well into the twentieth century. Then, as today, there was a considerable contrast in lifestyles between the officers and the enlisted ranks.

Because of this officer/enlisted distinction, in this history of military wives no woman stands solely on her own merit. She is either an officer's wife or an enlisted wife. The rank of her husband effects how she is perceived, whom her friends are, and where she lives. Although the woman may live on the same military base, the division between ranks is so sharp that even in the 1980s one wife would say, "It is as if a Berlin Wall were built between the two housing areas."

Historical references to military wives are sketchy. In fact one historian states, "Today one could read a hundred monographs on the American Revolution without getting more than a hint that women were involved at all."[6] When the women are mentioned, little is given about them that does not directly relate to the actions of their husbands. Also, notations in early biographies and autobiographies usually detail only the activities of wives of the higher ranking officers; almost nothing exists on the enlisted wife. The existing letters and diaries are those of officers' wives who were generally, it must be assumed, better educated than the wives of the enlisted men, and who also must have had more leisure time in which to write of their experiences.

Until the middle of the twentieth century, most wives of American soldiers remained behind, caring for children and property or living with relatives, while husbands fulfilled military obligations. During the Revolutionary War, however, many battles were fought within a few miles to a few hundred miles of the soldiers' homes. This made it possible for some wives to accompany their husbands from camp to camp or, in some cases, from battlefield to battlefield. Some wives became campfollowers to be near their loved ones or, in many instances, because of necessity. Once their husbands had joined the army, there was no one to stay with nor home to stay in. (At Camp Kimble near Morristown, during the winter of 1780-81, it was estimated that there were nearly 100 women and children—families of men who had no other way to provide for them).[7] Those who stayed behind suffered the loneliness of separation; those who followed suffered the hardships (and had the adventure) of travel, camp living, and separation when husbands went into the field. For the officers' wives, hardships could sometimes be eased; for the enlisted, they had to be endured.

The Americans had no policy actually forbidding women to follow. However, the closest the Continental Army came to officially condoning female participation in the war was the hiring of laundresses who washed and mended the soldiers' clothing. For their hard work these women received a campfollower's stipend of "half rations for themselves and quarter rations for each child."[8] Many times they were the wives of noncommissioned officers (NCOs) and, occasionally, of men in the lower enlisted ranks. Their presence in Continental Army camps is documented by references to orders warning them that they "must not throw soapsuds on the parade ground, that they must make use of the latrines and that they must not ride in the baggage wagons in the march."[9]

The maintenance of wives, other than laundresses, was the responsibility of the soldiers. No legal or official status was given to these women, and the ragtag Continental Army was under no obligation, nor was it economically able, to provide housing, transportation, or rations for them. Encampments were rife with dysentery and smallpox; food was often in short supply, a fact which Washington constantly emphasized in his letters to colony governors.[10] The military did not provide medical care for wives in case of accident, illness, or pregnancy, nor could it guarantee the safety of wives if an attack was made on an encampment or if they moved too close to battle lines. In point of fact, the Army did not want the women at camp, but since it did not forbid the practice, it seemed unable to settle the issue to the satisfaction of everyone.

In August 1777, as the Americans were moving south from New Jersey to meet the British threat to Philadelphia, General Washington became so concerned at the "multitude of women . . . especially those who are pregnant or have children" accompanying the Continental Army that he issued an order for his officers to control the problem by "getting rid of all such as are not absolutely necessary" and forbidding the admission of any additional wives to the ranks.[11]

The women, of course, were not happy with this directive. One wife, Mrs. Clement Biddle of Rhode Island (who was with her colonel husband in the Valley Forge encampment) decided to wage a subtle campaign against being sent home. After preparing a delicious dinner for General Washington and his staff, Mrs. Biddle rose from the dinner table and sweetly remarked that while she had heard of the order, she felt certain General Washington would not apply it to her. Apparently realizing that he had been taken in, the commander-in-chief bowed graciously and replied to her charming speech, "Certainly not."[12]

Over the course of the war many orders were issued that "the women who have children and all those unable to march on foot must also be sent off, as none will be permitted to ride on wagons or horses, on any pretext whatever."[13] In South Carolina, in 1780, while marching toward the enemy, General Horatio Gates ordered that at least a part of the women and children following the soldiers be sent back to Charlotte; however, the women ignored the order and "clung to their protectors."[14]

Most of the wives tended to disregard the orders, and the Army found it difficult to enforce them. The women were resourceful, and learned how to move in and out of camps. Then, too, they could always reside on the fringes of the encampments. Even when the proportion of women to men reached the one to fifteen ratio (the ratio of laundresses authorized by the Continental Congress), Washington was reluctant to order any wives out of camp for fear of troops deserting if their families were abandoned.[15]

It is fairly clear that a double standard existed when dealing with officer versus enlisted wives, as in the case of Mrs. Biddle. In addition, Washington, General Henry Knox, and a number of other higher ranking officers encouraged (or at least did not discourage wives) to accompany them. Most officers, of course, were better able to provide for wives and children; therefore, the tendency for them to become a burden or a nuisance for the Army was less than it was for the enlisted families. However, regardless of finances and Washington's wishes, wives of all ranks continued to join their husbands in the encampments.

OFFICERS' WIVES

One of the most famous early officers' wives to follow her husband was Martha Washington, who shuttled between the Washingtons' Mount Vernon plantation and various encampments. Every winter from 1776 until the signing of the peace found the general's lady with the troops. The places she visited, the people she encountered were far beyond the restricted world of the plantation lady. She spent the first winter in Craigie House, one of the famous mansions on Tory Row in Cambridge, Massachusetts. But in succeeding years her quarters were far less genteel. Wherever cold weather stopped the Army, there Martha Washington drove to from Virginia, her coach completely filled with cooked food from Mount Vernon.[16]

When the Continental Army moved into winter quarters, the officers' wives joined their men, some effortlessly, some with considerable difficulty. In December 1775, Martha Washington apparently arrived in Cambridge in a "four-horse carriage with a coachman . . . wearing the red and white Washington livery."[17] Catherine Littlefield Greene, wife of General Nathanael Greene, once joined her husband at his headquarters in Middlebrook, Virginia, after "a hazardous and almost ill-fated journey through the blizzards to reach camp only a short while before the birth of her fourth child."[18]

Many times an accurate picture is difficult to find because sources differ. For example, one source mentions that when Mrs. Washington made the trip to Valley Forge, "a heavy snow was falling as they set out on the long, cold journey, George riding his big bay horse, Martha behind him on a pillion."[19] She had to travel in a rough sleigh, another author writes, as heavy snow had forced her to abandon her coach.[20] Yet another source indicates that each fall Washington would send her notice to join him at his headquarters, and she would "arrive in a simple carriage with a few servants, bringing homespun garments for herself and needed clothes for George."[21] Regardless of her means of travel, Martha apparently spent a portion of each of the war years with the general.

Diaries and letters of those who came in contact with Mrs. Washington make her appear almost saintlike and commend her kindness, compassion, generosity, and humble personality. Joined by the wives of generals Gates, Greene, and Knox, Martha was seen by the public as the "idol for the war's women,"[22] or perhaps as a symbol of a "gallant, new American womanhood."[23]

With the aid of the other officers' wives, both at home and in the camps, she formed what may have been the forerunner of the Officers' Wives' Club (OWC) and the Family Services program. While these social gatherings provided a sense of camaraderie for the war-weary wives, they also were designed to help the war effort. Circles of women knitted and sewed for the troops, rolled bandages from cast-off linen, and helped care for the ill and wounded.

Mrs. Washington was particularly noted for her attempts to boost the morale of the men and to give medical aid when possible. One account tells of her entering "a dark, miserable room" at Valley Forge to feed broth to a dying sergeant and to bring comfort to his young wife who was at his bedside.[24]

A sixteen-year-old girl who saw Mrs. Washington in camp (and claimed to have occasionally accompanied her on her camp rounds) provided this account at age eighty:

> I never in my life knew a woman so busy from early morning until late at night as was Lady Washington, providing comfort for the sick soldiers. Every day, excepting Sundays, the wives of officers in camp . . . [assisted] her in knitting socks, patching garments, and making shirts for the poor soldiers when materials could be procured. . . . she

might be seen, with basket in hand . . . going among the
huts seeking the keenest and most needy sufferers, and
giving all the comfort to them in her power.[25]

Although Martha was not born to great wealth, her first
marriage gave her a considerable fortune, including Mount
Vernon. She adapted well to the rigors of camp life and, report-
edly, was not one to "put on airs." When the Marquis de
Chastellux, visiting Washington's camp at Morristown, New
Jersey, found Martha dressed in a plain russet gown with a white
handkerchief around her neck, he thought she was a domestic.[26]
When visiting ladies, bedecked in all their finery, entered the
Washingtons' cramped quarters at Freeman Tavern in Morristown, they were shocked to find that Martha had left her silks
and jewels behind. Dressed in brown homespun and a checked
apron, Martha explained to her visitors, "Our break with England
has cut us off from many of our necessities. . . . We women must
make ourselves independent [of England] . . . learn to do without
the things we cannot make at home."[27]

She reminded them of how important it was for American
women to realize the country was at war and to contribute what
they could to the war effort. Even though she was the wife of
General Washington, Martha thought of herself as just an "old
fashioned Virginia housewife, steady as a clock, busy as a bee,
and cheerful as a cricket."[28] By her actions and attitude, and
probably without being conscious of the effect on future generations, she set the standard for service and volunteerism which the
military would exact from wives over the next two centuries.

While Martha occasionally helped with Washington's correspondence, her chief concern apparently was to see to the
general's comfort and health during his time in the field. A good
example of her determination to care for her husband occurred
in early 1777. Encamped near Morristown, General Washington
became so ill from an attack of quinsy, a severe inflammation of
the throat with fever and swelling, that he asked General Greene
to succeed him if he should die. Several weeks later at Mount

Vernon, Martha learned of her husband's illness and wrote him a letter indicating that if she did not hear immediately of his recovery, she would be on her way to Morristown. "And if no carriage is available, I'll come on foot."[29] His answer, if there was one, apparently did not satisfy Martha for she was soon by his side.

Attempting to accommodate wives and families caused problems which have continued to plague the military up to the present. Providing housing for wives accompanying soldiers has always been difficult, and this was true for the Continental Army. Officers' wives could sometimes find quarters in private homes near their husbands' commands, but many times the quarters were crowded and uncomfortable, as the Washingtons learned when Isaac Potts permitted them use of two rooms on the ground floor of his home near Valley Forge. One room was the couple's bedroom/sitting room; the other was General Washington's command post.[30] Still, no complaint came from Martha Washington, one of the country's richest women, as she wrote to Mercy Warren of Boston, describing their housing as "tolerable comfortable."[31] Through the years, other military wives in dingy, cramped quarters would follow Martha's example and try uncomplainingly to make a "home away from home."

Unfortunately, not all Continental Army officers' wives consistently set as good an example as Martha Washington. Following the Battle of Trenton, an Elisha Hall, Jr. of Wallingford, Connecticut, wrote to General Knox, complaining that the general's wife, Lucy, and a Mrs. Pollard had damaged his property. Hall explained that since the two women did not have housing, he had taken pity on them, allowing them to live in his home. After they had stayed a month, he discovered that "all the crockery was broken, the furniture badly damaged, and twenty-five gallons of his best Indian rum had disappeared."[32] There is no indication of what General Knox did with this complaint nor of what he may have said to Lucy.

Normally for the officers' wives, life in or near camp was fairly placid, but accompanying a husband could occasionally turn out to be more hazardous than anticipated. In December 1775, while with General Washington at Cambridge, Massachusetts, Martha confessed in a letter to a friend at Mount Vernon that there was shelling near her quarters.

> Some days we have a number of shells from Boston and Bunker Hill, but it does not seem to surprise anyone but me. . . . I shuder [sic] every time I hear the sound of a gun . . . but I endever [sic] to keep my fears to myself as well as I can.[33]

Martha seldom ventured far from her quarters at Cambridge, not only because of the shelling, but because of the cold, gray climate. For one woman, the routine of wartime living at this camp was apparently a particularly dreary and depressing experience, for it is recorded that the wife of a Colonel Huntington became so depressed that she committed suicide.[34]

The wives not only had to survive dreary and depressing days but also life-threatening situations. Lucy Knox found herself in a somewhat dangerous position in the summer of 1776. One morning she and General Knox were enjoying breakfast at their quarters in New York City when the British fleet sailed into New York harbor. Although the general was aware of the "distress and anxiety Lucy had [with] the city in an uproar, the alarm guns firing, the troops repairing to their posts, and everything in the height of battle," he heeded the call to duty, left her to fend for herself, and went to his command post since "my country calls loudest."[35] If he was overly worried about abandoning Lucy, he made no notations to this effect. Later he did "scold her for not having left the city earlier,"[36] and shortly thereafter sent her back to New England.

Duty always came first as Catherine Greene, "a handsome, elegant and accomplished woman,"[37] found when trying to stay near General Greene. Tediously journeying from Rhode Island to West Point to join him, Catherine arrived only to learn that the general had been appointed as the new commander of the

Southern Army to replace General Gates. In a hurry to reach his new command, Greene had left West Point and missed her entirely. He did send a letter of apology later on.[38] Yet Martha, Lucy, and Catherine conquered or concealed their fears and annoyance, accepted the fact that they came second to the needs of the army and remained at their husbands' sides, as other American service wives would continue to do in the years to follow.

In spite of the rigors of Revolutionary War camplife, the tradition was being set for officers' wives to entertain for their husbands. (These ladies brightened drab camplife for officers only; if the enlisted wives entertained, they left no record of it.) General Washington hosted visiting dignitaries from foreign governments as well as other senior officers who were constantly at his headquarters and who had to be shown some degree of hospitality. Small dinners were given as Martha Washington strove to be a gracious hostess. Open house for his officers was held twice a week at Washington's headquarters; according to an old diary, "the General's lady seemed in perfect felicity by the side of her 'Old Man' as she occasionally called him."[39] Although there may appear to be a contradiction in the image of Martha as a "homespun housewife" and a "social butterfly," this is not the case. Apparently Martha's entertaining was fairly sedate and far from lavish. In the early years of the war (and specifically at Valley Forge), the shortage of rations meant that Martha's "refreshments many times consisted only of a dish of tea or coffee." These were not formal gatherings, and amusement was often limited to singing and conversation.[40]

Other officers' wives (particularly those of Washington's generals) also entertained. Catherine Greene was hostess at many lively parties, including one at her Valley Forge quarters, "a hut little larger than those in which the rank and file starved and froze."[41] Descriptions of dark-eyed Catherine indicate that she was a rare beauty, witty and vivacious and usually surrounded by admiring males. She was said once to have danced with General Washington "upwards of three hours without once sitting down."[42]   The parties of General Knox and Lucy were many times quite lavish, and they were described as "energetic, jovial individuals" who gave many a "gay frisk."[43]

Also with her husband at Valley Forge was Elizabeth Phillips Gates, the wife of General Horatio Gates. The daughter of an army officer and apparently quite ambitious, Elizabeth Gates did her share of entertaining and hoped by doing so to further her husband's career. However, a quarrel Elizabeth had with Martha Washington during a social event may have hindered more than helped the general's advancement.[44] Then, as today, it was not politically astute to offend the wife of an officer who outranked your husband.

ENLISTED WIVES

Wives of enlisted men also swelled the ranks of the army, but with few exceptions they shared a wretched and sometimes dangerous existence. Unlike the generals' wives who usually traveled in some comfort, these women, and especially the laundresses, followed the Army on foot, "weighed down with heavy iron pots, small children and baggage."[45] Another description of the women accompanying the troops notes that they were "bedraggled creatures, their faces blackened by the smoke of campfires, their backs bent under heavy loads as they straggled along with savage and unkempt brats."[46]

Of course, the women tagging along gave the Continental Army a very unprofessional appearance. Once, in an effort to remedy this problem and spruce up the column's image before the soldiers marched to the Battle of Brandywine, Washington issued an order that "not a woman belonging to the Army is to be seen with the troops."[47] Apparently the order was not carried out, as a Philadelphian described the appearance of the women as they accompanied the men, "their hair flying, their brows beady with the heat, their belongings slung over one sholder [sic], chattering and yelling sluttish shrills as they went and spitting in the gutter."[48]

Quarters were seldom available for wives of enlisted men, and to get shelter they were forced (and permitted) to sleep with the troops in tents or huts. Most of the enlisted wives had little money and foraged for food for their children, themselves, and their husbands. Many times they looted and stripped the dead for needed supplies. However, neither daily hardships nor the possibilities of rape, injury from battle, or widowhood deterred the women. If an enlisted woman's husband died or was killed, often she had little choice but to attach herself to another trooper; for many there was no longer a home to which they could return.[49] While officers' wives, who for the most part were financially more secure, accompanied husbands because they wished to, the enlisted wives followed because their only "home" might be their husbands' encampment. If an officer was killed, usually family or other officers escorted his widow safely home; the enlisted wife fended for herself.

As with Martha Washington and Lucy Knox, enlisted wives could not automatically be sent to safety when the shooting began. Occasionally, some were involved in battles and reacted heroically. Mary Ludwig Hays (better known as Molly Pitcher, a name common to many of the women who carried water to the men in battle) actually assisted her enlisted husband, artilleryman John Hays, in firing his cannon. In fact, she "fired the last cannon shot prior to the fall of Fort Clinton in 1777."[50] Later Mary, her pregnancy far advanced, accompanied Hays to Monmouth, New Jersey, where she carried water to the soldiers in battle. When her husband collapsed, either from a bullet wound or heat exhaustion, Molly is said to have "singlehandedly sponged, loaded, aimed and fired the cannon in addition to nursing her husband." Private Joseph Martin recorded the following incident in his diary:

One little incident happened, during the heat of the cannonade, which I was eye witness to. . . . While in the act of reaching for a cartridge and having one of her [Molly's] feet as far before the other as she could step, a cannon shot from the enemy passed directly between her legs without doing any other damage than carrying away all the lower part of her petticoat. Looking at it with apparent unconcern, she observed that it was lucky it did not pass a little higher, for in that case it might have carried away something else, and continued her occupation.[51]

It is said that General Greene located Molly and presented her to Washington, who gave her a gold coin and promoted her to sergeant. Supposedly, she was dubbed "Captain Molly," and as she would pass along the lines, French soldiers serving with the Americans would fill her cocked hat with silver coins.[52] Years later she was awarded a pension of half-pay for life.[53]

Today, in a cemetery in Carlisle, Pennsylvania, there is a statue honoring Molly Pitcher, with the following words carved at her feet:

> O'er Monmouth's field of carnage drear
> With cooling drink and words of cheer
> A woman passed who knew no fear
> The wife of Hays, the gunner. . . .
> From the ranks this woman came
> By the cannon won her fame:
> 'Tis true she could not write her name
> But freedom's hand hath carved it.
>   Sarah Woods Parkinse

A few words record the deeds of another enlisted wife, twenty-five-year-old Margaret Cochran Corbin (sometimes also called Molly or Captain Molly), who followed her husband to Fort Washington, New York. When he was wounded, like Mary Hays she took up his musket and continued firing until she had one of her arms almost severed and her breast laced by grape-shot.[54] In 1779, she was rewarded by the State of Pennsylvania with a small grant of $30, and Congress approved the following resolution:

Resolved: That Margaret Corbin who was wounded and disabled in the attack on Fort Washington, whilst she heroically filled the post of her husband who was killed by her side serving a piece of artillery, do receive, during her natural life . . . the one-half of the monthly pay drawn by a soldier in the service of these states.[55]

Brief mention is also made of a pension request for an Anna Maria Lane, wife of soldier John Lane, who was, apparently, severely disabled "by a wound, which she received while fighting as a common soldier, in one of our Revolutionary battles from which she never has recovered, and perhaps never will recover."[56] (It is not known if Anna Maria received the pension.)

Disease, famine, and danger were ever present, and sometimes the wives did not survive. In November 1775, two wives accompanied 1,000 rebel soldiers, led by Benedict Arnold, from Fort Western near the mouth of the Kennebec River in Maine to attack Quebec. One, described as a large woman, was Mrs. Grier, the wife of a Pennsylvania sergeant; the other was Jemima Warner, wife of Private James Warner. During the march, the army encountered unexpected swamps, many men contracted dysentery and pneumonia, and the food supply became so low that the troops ate the company dog, shaving soap, and shoe leather. Private Warner soon lagged behind the rest of the men, who could not wait for him. Jemima stayed by his side until he died, then took his gun and other implements and rejoined the company. On April 18, 1776, note was made that "a woman of the Pennsylvania troops was killed today by accident—a soldier carelessly snapping his musket, which proved fatal." It was not known whether this was Mrs. Grier, Mrs. Warner, or some other woman who may have joined the troops at a later time.[57]

Nor were activities of Revolutionary War wives confined solely to the North. After learning her husband had been in a battle, Mary Slocum, a North Carolina planter's wife, saddled her mare and rode forty miles at night to the battlefield where her husband had been fighting. Before learning late in the day that her husband was safe, she had helped tend many of the wounded. Then, after a brief reunion with her spouse, Mary galloped home to care for the infant she had left with a servant woman.[58]

With records on Revolutionary War enlisted wives almost nonexistent, little else is known of Mary Slocum or her husband. The more detailed information on Mary Ludwig and Margaret Corbin appears in old records, apparently because of their government pensions. However, these sparse bits of documentation show that, like the officers' wives, the enlisted wives endured the military lifestyle and gave support to their Continental Army husbands.

ASSETS OR LIABILITIES?

Were the wives assets or liabilities? Even in historical records, this issue is debated. Women lagged during marches, slowing troop movements. There are indications that some women, alone and unable to support themselves or their children, persuaded soldiers to desert.[59]

Regardless of her wifely contributions at Valley Forge, General Charles Lee spoke of Elizabeth Gates as "that Medusa . . . [who] governs with a rod of Scorpions."[60] While Lucy Knox was said by one author to have boosted morale with her "lively disposition and boundless energy [which] helped brighten the drabness of Valley Forge,"[61] another source described her as "meddlesome, extravagant and constantly berating Henry for inconveniences caused by the conflict. . . . and aware of the sacrifices she was making on behalf of the cause."[62] During a stay in Connecticut, she grumbled that the family who had given her refuge was too common for her tastes and "as unrefined as yeomanry."[63]

Even the sacrifices of Martha Washington are dimmed when one learns that the General sent a bill for $27,665.30 to Congress for Martha's "travell [sic] Exps. in coming to & returning from my Winter Quarters per accts. rendered.—The Money to defray which being taken from my private Purse & brought with her from Virginia."[64]

On the other hand, Mrs. Biddle made herself extremely useful as she foraged for food for the troops.[65] Catherine Greene helped interpret for the French troops who were fighting with the Continental Army at Valley Forge.[66] Having Martha near was a great boost to Washington's morale as her visits brought "in addition to companionship, a feeling of his hearth, a sense that he was breathing the air of home. . . . he could almost forget the war."[67]

Washerwomen often were Washington's most effective spies (many of them also did laundry in or near enemy camps).[68] In addition, both officer and enlisted wives brought to encampments food, clothing, and news of home, and nursed the sick and wounded.

Margaret Catherine Moore Barry, wife of Captain Andrew Barry, was an accomplished horsewoman and sometimes scouted for General Daniel Morgan. "Kate" often alerted the forces to impending British attacks. She was accorded the title "heroine of Cowpens" for bringing the South Carolina Rangers to bolster Morgan's troops and help defeat Tarleton and his British legion on January 15, 1781.[69] "Kate Barry's Famous Ride," a poem by H. R. Wilkins, calls her "a prototype of those who fought for the Cause of Liberty" and ranks her along with other patriots of that period.[70]

Whether or not they considered themselves prototypes, wives were determined to accompany their husbands and to give what aid and comfort they could. For some wives of the Continental Army, this lifestyle continued after the British surrender. A great continent was opening up, and army wives were determined to follow their soldier husbands westward toward the Mississippi and become a part of the great adventure.

CHAPTER TWO

EYES WEST:
1780–1850

Mrs. Duffy gazed with compassion at the young soldier as he was carried into her barrack room at Fort McIntosh. While ferrying rations to the frontier force along the Ohio River, he had fallen into the icy water. His frozen legs and feet badly needed medical attention. Mrs. Duffy's room (which she shared with her sergeant major husband and another corporal) was the only hospital quarters available. The patient survived, due almost entirely to the nursing of Mrs. Duffy and the wife of Colonel Josiah Harmar, perhaps the first American regular army wives to appear in military records.[1]

These two wives were part of the military which remained in uniform after the surrender of the British at Yorktown. Most of the Continental Army had returned to civilian life, leaving only a small cadre of men in a standing army. Fearful that the military might become "an active agent in establishing despotism," Congress in 1784 discharged all troops except fifty-five men at West Point and twenty-five at Fort Pitt.[2] However, exploration of the continent had continued even during the Revolutionary War, and as explorers, trappers, and settlers steadily pushed farther into a hostile interior, they looked to the military for protection.

Resenting the intrusion of immigrants, Indians were raiding along the northwestern frontier in Ohio and Pennsylvania and in Kentucky and Tennessee. "The Cumberland settlements, never with any proper fort or paid soldiers, knew Indian raids almost weekly for fifteen years."[3] In June 1784, reacting to Indian hostilities, Congress asked Connecticut, New York, New Jersey, and Pennsylvania for 700 men "to act as garrisons and to furnish protection to the country north of the Ohio."[4] This was the beginning of the regular army—those men who would carve careers from years of continued military service.

A regiment theoretically numbered nearly 900 men, but most usually averaged 300–400. Companies within a regiment should have had 100 men, but many were composed of 1 or 2 officers and 30–40 troopers.[5] These companies were scattered at scores of small outposts, and the army seldom had adequate numbers to fulfill its duties.

In 1833, as Americans pushed farther into the interior, the defense of the frontier followed a sort of half circle, with troops at Fort Howard in Green Bay, Fort Snelling on the Upper Mississippi, Fort Leavenworth on the Missouri near the Little Platte River, and some cantonments in Louisiana. Estimated strength of all of these forts in 1835 was 2,421 enlisted men and 151 officers, making the army guarding the West "little more than a tiny and widely scattered police force."[6] Nevertheless, the army focused its energies on westward expansion, establishing fortresses, and challenging the wilderness.

Post–Revolutionary War garrisons were mostly male. Inadequate pay to support a family was a major reason why most enlisted men and many officers failed to marry. At the end of the War of 1812, enlisted pay ranged from $5 a month for private, the lowest enlisted rank, to $9 a month for a sergeant major, the highest enlisted rank. By 1854, a sergeant major earned $20 a month.

First lieutenants' pay was better, ranging from $60 to $75 a month, but there was little chance for improvement as promotions were extremely slow.[7] An officer could spend twenty to thirty years reaching the rank of major: one West Point graduate of 1826 was promoted to major in 1857.[8] However, life was not monastic for all. A few soldiers were accompanied by wives and children, and the camp laundresses were always present.

The position of females in camp was a tenuous one and subject to the whims of those in charge. Colonel Jonas Simonds directed that any soldier in his command contemplating marriage must have approval of his company commander (a practice that continued into the twentieth century), and ordered that only those women and children "who had been certified by officers" would be admitted on boats carrying the Sixth Infantry from Pennsylvania to Mississippi. On the other hand, in 1797, General James Wilkinson had acknowledged dependents' needs by authorizing a ration to each child and an extra ration for mothers suckling infants.[9] As during the Revolutionary War, enforcing restrictions against families accompanying soldiers was nearly impossible. When the men marched, so did the women.

For example, in 1791, when Major General Arthur St. Clair's command of 1,700 men prepared to march toward Fort Washington near Greenville, Ohio, an enormous caravan resulted. Traveling with the soldiers in columns of carts were 200 or more females—washerwomen (4 were allowed to each company), wives (some pregnant, some with babies), and mistresses.[10] These women would not have met the conventional standards set in those days for "ladies." Most tended to be robust and sometimes earthy and profane, but they were not, for the most part, prostitutes. Like their counterparts of the American Revolution, they were both officer and enlisted wives, some of whom accepted government pay and rations for doing camp laundry, nursed the sick and wounded and, when necessary, bravely fought beside their men. The treks were long and arduous, the camps cold and dreary, and the food often unfit for human consumption.[11] Only the hardiest survived for any length of time.

TREKS, TOMAHAWKS, AND TYPHUS

Danger was their constant companion. In one of General St. Clair's battles with Indians, along the Wabash River in Ohio, women fought "like furies, shaming the cowards among the men."[12] During the fight, only three escaped death with the rest

"inhumanly butchered, with every indecent and aggravated cir-
cumstance of cruelty." One soldier fleeing from the battle came
across a Corporal Mott and "a tall, strong woman known as
'Red-headed Nance' . . . both weeping bitterly; the corporal had
lost his wife and the woman her child."[13]

Lydia Bacon, who had accompanied her soldier husband to
Indiana in 1811, was only one of many wives who was fearful of
the Indian tribes. When the troops left Vincennes for the Battle
of Tippecanoe during the War of 1812, she admitted in a letter to
her mother that she rarely wandered far from home "for I do not
like the thought of being scalped by our red Brethren."[14]

In 1812, the Indians attacked a column of settlers and military
families that was under a Potowatamie guarantee of safe escort
from Fort Dearborn to Fort Wayne. The soldiers, under the
command of Captain Nathan Heald, attempted to defend the
wagons but were soon overrun. The women defended themselves
and their children but many were killed, including Rebekah
Heald's Negro slave, Cicely, and Susan and Victoria Corbin,
wives of Privates James and Phelim Corbin. Mary Cooper
Burns, Martha Lee, Sarah Neads, Jane Holt, and Susan Milhouse
Simmons, all wives of enlisted men, were taken captive by the
Indians, as were Mrs. Heald and Margaret McKillips Helm, wife
of Lieutenant Linai T. Helm. Although most of the women were
subsequently rescued or ransomed, Sarah Neads died of starva-
tion and exposure while still in captivity.[15]

In addition to the captured women having to watch their
husbands being slaughtered, they also had to witness the bloody
deaths of their children. Both of the children of Victoria and
Phelim Corbin were killed, as was the eight-month fetus ripped
from Victoria's womb by the attackers. An Indian youth leaped
into the wagon containing the younger children and, using a
tomahawk, killed many of them—Cicely's year-old son, the
three-year-old and six-year-old sisters of Isabella Cooper (who
he had previously struck down but who was still alive), and
two-year-old David Simmons. "The bloodstained Indian youth
. . . completed his grisly work by scalping the seven dead chil-

dren and throwing their lifeless bodies outside, where they fell to the ground as if they were lifeless dolls."[16]

In 1813, along the Alabama River, fear of a Creek Indian uprising prodded nearly 500 people to seek refuge at Fort Mims, which was not a military fort but a stockade belonging to a Samuel Mims. Major Daniel Beasley took command of the fort with 175 territorial militia to provide protection. Unfortunately, Major Beasley left the gates open during the day so that the occupants could move freely outside the confining walls. Scoffing at reports of Indian sightings, which he thought were just of herds of cattle, he and the rest of the people in the fort sat down to their noon meal on August 29. With a yell, Creeks rushed the fort killing nearly everyone, including most of the women and children.[17] Certainly, living with the constant fear of Indian attack must have challenged both the emotional and physical strength of the frontier military family.

Even without Indian attacks, travel and the daily rigors of garrison life took a heavy toll on families. In 1820, shortly after Colonel Josiah Snelling established Fort Snelling on the forks of the St. Peter and Mississippi rivers, Abigail Snelling followed her husband to the fort, as did several other officers' wives. One of them, Mary Henderson Eastman, wife of Captain Seth Eastman, kept a journal and wrote romantically of the fort, referring to the "excitement, the charm of garrison life." Life could not have been entirely charming, however, for the Snellings lost a thirteen-month-old daughter shortly after the family settled at the fort, and Lieutenant and Mrs. Platt Green's baby died soon thereafter.[18]

Disease was not discriminatory. It did not attack only children. Young women were especially vulnerable, and many soldiers became young widowers. Records from Fort Towson and Fort Gibson in Oklahoma Territory also report the untimely deaths of many military wives. In January 1836 at Fort Towson, Charlotte C. Voxe (daughter of the fort's commandant) wed Lieutenant Thomas C. Barnwell; on September 9 the young bride was dead. Then in July 1843, Virginia L. Beall (daughter of the fort's commandant) married John D. Bacon; she died the next year. Flora M. Coodey, "a beautiful seventeen-year-old," married Lieutenant D. H. Rucker during his early service at Fort Gibson. On June 26, 1845, at the age of twenty-one years and five months, she was dead.[19] Cholera broke out at Fort Leavenworth in 1848, and an epidemic of dysentery nearly immobilized the garrison another year.[20] Although many of the records do not indicate cause of death for specific women, typhus, diphtheria, pneumonia, and complications of childbirth were high on the list. The remoteness of the frontier and the great lonely distance between oases of civilization hindered access to what medical care might have been available.

While not every experience was life threatening, many required considerable stamina. In 1816, Harriet Lovejoy, third wife of Lieutenant Colonel Henry Leavenworth, and her daughter decided to join Leavenworth (newly appointed Indian agent for the Northwest Territory) at his post on the Wisconsin River near its confluence with the Mississippi. Little did they realize what this trip would entail. From New Orleans they journeyed to St. Louis, where fourteen "polite and obliging" Indians were waiting to carry them over 700 miles in a palanquin (a covered litter on poles). Harriet and her daughter are believed to have been the first white women to have made this 34-day trip through untamed wilderness.[21]

Perhaps most women were not as eager to join their husbands as Harriet was (or they could not get permission or money to do so), for the farther west the army moved, the fewer the women accompanied them. This changed dramatically after the Civil War, but in the early part of the nineteenth century, wives and families were exceptions on frontier posts. For example, in 1827, records show that only three military wives were at Cantonment Leavenworth, west of present day Kansas City.[22]

For those who did follow their husbands, some of their treks are almost too rigorous for belief. In June 1819, the Fifth Infantry, led by Lieutenant Colonel Leavenworth, rowed up the Fox-Wisconsin river accompanied by two officers' wives, one of whom was in her last month of pregnancy. Labor pains began as the party arrived at Prairie du Chien. The troops camped and waited until Lieutenant Nathan Clark's wife gave birth to a daughter. Then, with the two wives and the newborn infant in tow, the company continued to the mouth of the St. Peter's River. While the soldiers labored for several months constructing a temporary stockade containing forty-five separate quarters for officers, their families, and the enlisted ranks, the two women lived in the boats.[23] Although there is no specific record as to how these families reacted to their lifestyle, surely they must have been ecstatic to leave the small boats for quarters—quarters which at these early forts were mostly austere, dirty, and cramped.

HOMES OR HOVELS

Housing for wives and families was a continuing problem. In the early days at established posts in the East, such as Fort Monroe, Virginia, some space for a few quarters had been made in the stone and brick casemates (armored compartments for artillery). These usually consisted of two rooms, a front room and a bedroom, heated by a double fireplace and with only a small window at each end for ventilation. Cooking facilities were not always available and meals for the entire family had to be taken at nearby boarding houses or hotels.[24] Although many times damp and dreary, casemate housing could be considered gracious living compared to conditions on the frontier.

Philippe Regis de Trobriand, a Frenchman who had fought in the Revolutionary War and remained a colonel in the United States Army, tells in his journal of living conditions at Fort Steven, Dakota Territory. Several of the officers' families were housed in quarters built of logs and mud. Roofs were primitively made of sod, which continually dropped bits of earth or dust onto the furniture and occupants. Snow was another problem. De Trobriand recounts the tale of Lieutenant and Mrs. R. Frank Walborn. An avalanche broke down the door of their hut and filled all the living area except the kitchen, where the Walborns and their two small children stayed until they could be dug out. Shortly after, a warm spell caused the remnants of snow left in the quarters to melt and run down the walls and over the floor.[25]

Fleas and ants were the scourge of Teresa Griffin Viele during her years on the Texas frontier in the 1850s. In 1852, at Fort Brown near Brownsville, Texas, she decided:

> This portion of the world may be set down as the birthplace of the flea; those found in other parts are merely occasional wanderers from this, their native land. Here they run at large, the torment, par excellence, of the human race, in consequence of which carpets are eschewed, as they are apt to furnish a resort for scores of fleas, as well as other vermin of the country.[26]

At Ringgold Barracks along the Rio Grande River, Teresa found red ants "so thick that it was impossible to eat without devouring them by the scores." After a while, Mrs. Viele apparently became accustomed to eating the ants, for she indicated that they tasted a little like caraway seeds and "were not as disagreeable as a novice might suppose."[27]

In the interior, before posts were constructed, families (especially enlisted) slept in the open, shared tents with the men, or found shelter in dugouts and caves. While a few of the top-grade enlisted men had their families with them, generally quarters were provided only for commissioned officers. An enlisted man with dependents was forced to build a rough cabin or purchase one from a departing family. "Even with the extra money their wives earned by doing laundry, an enlisted man could hardly afford a spouse, for infantry privates got only eleven dollars a month. . . . pay could be in arrears as long as six months."[28]

As the army settled into newly constructed forts, it maintained the separation of officer and enlisted ranks. Having been granted legal status as army laundresses by an act of Congress in 1802, these laundresses were described as "red-armed wives . . . [with] broods of unkempt urchins who raced around the big black

laundry kettles that bubbled over woodfires in the backyards of
Suds Row shanties."[29] Usually quartered in small cabins located
away from officers' quarters and beyond the company barracks,[30]
theirs must have been a bleak existence of unrelieved drudgery.

Of course, housing (mainly for officers) on some garrisons was
better than on others, especially as the forts along the Ohio and
Mississippi Rivers became more established in the 1830s and
1840s. One record shows that by the summer of 1833, Fort
Towson's officers' quarters were lathed and plastered, each with
a brick chimney and a piazza in front and back. It was felt "that
there is not a better cantonment (built of wood) on the frontier."[31]
At Fort Leavenworth in 1846, the officers' quarters were well built
if not spacious. They were furnished mainly with cupboards made
of crates and boxes, heated in the winter with a sheet-iron stove
in the middle of the living room, which required that the weekly
bath be taken as close to the stove as possible.[32] Wives had to use
a great deal of ingenuity to make the quarters attractive or even
habitable.

One problem that began in the early days of the frontier army
and continued to irritate officers' wives well into the twentieth
century was the practice of being "ranked out" of quarters, known
by many as "falling bricks." It worked on this principle: If an
officer of a higher rank was assigned to the fort, he and his family
could "bump" a junior officer from his quarters. Many times
wives spent months settling into nearly unlivable quarters, decorating as best they could and planting a garden, only to have some
higher ranking officer's family reap the harvest.[33]

LEISURE AND "LUXURIES"

Although the women, like their soldier husbands, had to face
the hazards of Indian attack, disease, inclement weather and
inadequate housing, life in these beginning days of westward
expansion was not entirely without pleasant aspects. It was not
unusual for the officers' wives to enjoy the luxury of a household
servant—an Indian or mestizo woman (some of the latter early

French trapper's descendants)—since many officers continued to have economic resources other than their military salaries. White domestics (even very unattractive ones) were difficult to retain due to the shortage of women on the frontier and the demand for wives. Frances Mullen Boyd, wife of Lieutenant Orsemus Boyd, lamented her loss of a nursemaid, after deliberately choosing a particularly homely one:

> The girl was almost a grenadier in look and manners, and although not absolutely hideous, was so far from pleasing that we were confident of retaining her services. . . . she had not been in the fort three days before the man who laid our carpets proposed to her.[34]

However, even with a servant, frontier life in military posts was several levels below that of the more civilized East.

As the garrisons became established, some of the "luxuries" of life could be had, again chiefly for the officers' wives. In the late 1780s at Fort Harmar on the Muskingum River, officers' wives had planted petunias, cockscombs, four-o'clocks, and zinnias. "They had brought the seeds with them from the East; bright blossoms made the hardships of the wilderness less difficult to bear."[35]

Army regulations helped provide officers with some comfort by authorizing a baggage allowance "ranging from 500 pounds for lieutenants to 1,000 pounds for a major general."[36] While stationed at Fort McIntosh, Mrs. Josiah Harmar was able to receive from her Philadelphia home two armed Windsor chairs and six Windsor sidechairs to make her frontier quarters more comfortable.[37] Colonel Zachary Taylor had fine furniture and table service for his quarters at Fort Howard in 1816, and a piano could be found at Fort Snelling, brought there by Major Joseph C. Plympton.[38] Some of the early quarters of the officers' wives at Fort Snelling showed the ingenuity of the women who had made them into attractive homes for their husbands, and after being entertained by the Snellings, Major Stephen Long described their home as "almost elegant."[39] Of course, "elegant" on the frontier was a relative term.

Military families did find time to relax, entertain, and be entertained. At Fort Washington, Ohio, early in 1792, Brigadier General James Wilkinson and Mrs. Wilkinson had a "most sumptuous dinner" for the "principal officers, most respectable citizens, and a small but genteel female group." The guests dined in a huge wigwam which Wilkinson had erected especially for the occasion.[40]

Lieutenant Platt Green was even more enterprising in his efforts at relaxation. In 1823, at Fort Snelling, he built a summer cottage near Lake Calhoun, which became known as Green's Villa. Officers and their ladies invited to the villa were treated to picnics and game shooting, with the ladies attended by their husbands and by any other available unattached officers.[41]

With the scarcity of women on the frontier, weddings were always a big event, and letters and diaries tell of these special occasions. When a double wedding in 1846 at Fort Towson united Catherine Mix with Lieutenant Kirkham and Donna McMullen with Lieutenant Franklin F. Flint, the celebration was described in detail:

> The brides in their muslin dresses and veils rode in the only carriage at the post, a victoria holding two persons. The bridegrooms in full uniform walked along beside the carriage while the band outside the chapel played "Come haste to the wedding!" A reception was then held at the Colonel's house.[42]

For the frontier soldier these small, female-oriented social events must have added a homey touch to existence in an almost totally male environment.

HELP OR HINDRANCE?

However, while some men were anxious to have their wives with them (Captain Randolph Marcy frequently wrote anecdotes about "my dear wife" as Mrs. Marcy accompanied him during the 1830s and 1840s[43]), not everyone was content with having women at these early posts. Writing in 1829, shortly after leaving St. Louis and embarking on a Mississippi riverboat, Lieutenant Colonel Philip St. George Cooke comments on his surprise at the number of married men who had been selected to fill the company roster. He indicated his displeasure at the boat deck swarming with wives and squalling children on their way to join husbands and fathers.[44]

One enlisted man, Trumpeter Drawn of the Second Dragoons, commented in 1857 that wives did not realize the trouble they caused when traveling with the troops.

> Ask a soldier which he would rather have to wait upon, one woman or five horses, and he will tell you the horses by all odds. I don't believe ladies know the trouble they are on a march, to a body of troops, or they would stay home, where they ought to be, in time of war at least. . . . "God bless the ladies," I say, and keep them out of the way of hostile savages; but as long as they travel with troops they must necessarily be attended to as they cannot attend to themselves.[45]

Occasionally the women caused problems and had to be disciplined. For example, at Fort Gratiot, a Mrs. Innis was considered "a great nuisance for a long time" and was ordered to move her tent close to the guardhouse. Rather than do that, she chose to leave the fort.[46] Obviously, the actions of disruptive wives tended to reflect on all wives and created the impression that all were a nuisance.

Sergeant Major Theodore Talbot's evaluation of campfollowing wives, however, may be the most common opinion:

> We have about a score of soldiers' wives, who go out as company laundresses and who manage to make themselves as troublesome as all the rest of the command put together,

but I suppose they are necessary appurtenances to a military colony.[47]

On the other hand, there are also accounts of great service being performed by the wives. At the seige of Bryant's Station (near what is now Lexington, Kentucky) in August 1782, women are credited with saving the day. Realizing Indians were lying in wait to attack, but badly in need of the water which the wives lugged from the river each day, the men decided the women should continue their routine. "If the Indians saw them proceeding as usual, they would believe that their ambush still remained undiscovered. They would not unmask their positions to fire at a few women."[48] The women bravely brought back the water and completely deceived the Indians.

During the Mexican War, under bombardment at Corpus Christi, Texas, laundress/cook Sarah Boginnis (also listed under the surnames Bordinnis, Bourget, Bourdette, and Bouget) left the protection of the storage magazines and "oblivious to gunfire, cooked breakfast in the open courtyard, serving it on time complete with hot coffee."[49] Her judgment might be questioned, but not her heroism.

While these heroics in battle may have been rare, those few women who plodded westward during the years between the Revolutionary War and the Civil War were truly unsung heroines. Some died; many survived under harsh circumstances. However, they established the tradition of the self-sacrificing military wife who would carry with her a bit of "home" and create in the isolated, male outposts of the West a vestige of the civilization of the East.

CHAPTER THREE

STRIFE BETWEEN SISTERS: 1860–1865

In the midst of this period of economic expansion and westward movement, the nation was torn apart by the Civil War. As more than 2 million civilians donned the blue and gray uniforms of the North and South, women were again faced with the decision of whether to remain behind or follow their husbands to encampments and battlefields.[1] The situation for these wives was little different from their Revolutionary War counterparts. The military still took no responsibility for dependents; camp living was wretched; farms and homes needed tending. The women who stayed behind did so for a variety of reasons: some were abandoned, some needed to maintain a farm or plantation while husbands were gone, some could find no one to care for young children. Other women joined their men because either they had no choice or they wanted to be with and care for them.

The decision to follow the army to war must have taken enormous strength for many wives; however, if they lost their homes because of unpaid bills or were displaced by the advancing armies, often they had no alternative but to go directly to the camps to join their husbands.[2] For others, the decision may have been simply a logical one involving survival. If they stayed at home, they lived with the very real fear of invaders and little or no protection. Judith W. McGuire, in describing raids on civilian property, wrote in her *Diary of a Southern Refugee During the War* (published 1889) that the Federals

will ride bravely up to a house, where they will find only
women and children; order meals to be prepared; search the
house; take the valuables; feed their horses at the barns; take
off the horses from the stables; shoot the pigs, sheep and
other stock and leave them dead in the fields; rob the
poultry-yards; then, after regaling themselves on the meals
which have been prepared by force, with the threats of
bayonets and pistols, they ride off, having pocketed the silver
spoons and forks, which may have been unwittingly left in
their way.[3]

Many of the Civil War wives who followed their husbands did
so not because of desperation or threat but out of dedication and
affection. They, like wives of all ages, wanted to keep the family
together. Some, like the famous fictional Marmee in Louisa May
Alcott's *Little Women*, came to help nurse their injured husbands
back to health. Others served the war effort more directly as
couriers, bringing information and materiel to their men. Of
course, for hundreds of others the motivation may not have been
as noble. Some were merely lonely and bored. Some simply did
not trust their men after reading newspaper accounts of drinking,
gambling, and immorality. Many had heard or read that prosti-
tution was rampant. According to one correspondent, Washington, D.C. "was the most pestiferous hole since the days of Sodom
and Gomorrah."[4] Regardless of the reasons the wives had for
following, once they arrived in camp they faced the same crushing
problems as did their predecessors of 1776; their reasons for being
there tended to get lost in their scramble for survival.

As with the Revolutionary War, battles between the North and
South were often fought in nearby states or on home territory.
Only this time the enemy was not a foreign one. Men who had
been neighbors, friends, or business associates were now the foe.
While it was known as a war of brother against brother, it was
also a war of sister against sister. Women from both sides who
may have shared extended visits in each others' homes were now
contemplating joining husbands at war with each other.

Compared to the Revolutionary era, Civil War wives could join their husbands in towns or encampments near the battlefields—or on the battlefields themselves—in a relatively short time. Travel had become easier in the first half of the nineteenth century. Many new roads had been constructed, and old ones were improved; railroads criss-crossed the countryside in the East; and refurbished ports aided travel by boat.

Whether they stayed home or kept up with their husbands, life was not easy for women on either side. Money was tight, pay was often in arrears, and money sent home (sometimes to help wives join their husbands) frequently did not reach the wives. A Yankee private or corporal still earned only $11 a month; a sergeant, $20; a captain, $130; a colonel, $195; a brigadier general, $210.[5] Yet inadequate funds did not deter many of the wives. In Richmond after the Battle of Bull Run, it was said that "from all quarters of the Confederacy wives had followed their husbands to the scene of action, filling with other refugees every available boarding house, public and private in the city."[6] Mary Chesnut, wife of Colonel (later Brigadier General) James Chesnut, Jr., was among these women. Well educated, beautiful, and from a wealthy family, she joined her husband in Richmond in June 1861, and mentioned in her extensive diary of the war years the problems of finding housing. For years she, like many of the other wives, lived out of a trunk in rented rooms as she attempted to fulfill social and other duties connected with her husband's job.[7]

GOING TO WAR

A popular song of the times, "Cruel War," contains a verse in which a women pleads to accompany her "Johnny." Repeatedly the husband (or lover) denies her request. However, many wives ignored the men's protestations against following them to war and headed for their husbands' sides.

Living conditions in Civil War camps were deplorable as well as dangerous. In 1863, one officer's wife sent her two children to stay with an aunt and begged to be allowed to join her husband.

Permission was granted, and she was taken to a large battery outside of Charleston, South Carolina. For sixty days and nights she stayed with him, sharing his meager rations of wormy bread and half-cured pork and sipping brackish water from the ditch surrounding the earthwork. Artillery fired day and night; sleep was impossible. "But at length she became used to the cannonade and enjoyed intermittent slumbers, from which she was sometimes awakened by the explosion of a shell which had penetrated the roof of the fort and strewed the earth with dead and wounded."[8]

Union officers' wives were also literally "under the gun." Take the case of young Belle (Arabella) Reynolds, wife of Lieutenant William S. Reynolds of the Seventeenth Regiment of the Illinois Volunteers, who began a journal with the description of her living conditions in an 1861 camp at Bird's Point, Missouri:

> How could I stay in such a cheerless place? No floors, no chairs, the narrow cot my seat, my feet imbedded in the hot sand, the confusion of camp close around me, with but the thickness of cloth between me and the eyes of all.[9]

These conditions must have been particularly distressing for Belle, who had come from an economically comfortable family in Shelburne Falls, Massachusetts, and was accustomed to the comforts of the East.

Continuing her journal in 1862, after the battle of Shiloh, Mrs. Reynolds recounted cannonballs howling over her head while she (and another wife identified only as Mrs. N.) prepared breakfast for her husband. "Knowing my husband must go, I kept my place before the fire, that he might have his breakfast." With shells and musketballs coming ever nearer she still "fried my cakes and rollin [sic] them in a napkin, placed them in his haversack, and gave it to him just as he was mounting his horse to assist in forming the regiment."[10]

After her husband had ridden off, Belle was alarmed to see Rebel troops on a nearby hill. Both she and Mrs. N. returned to their tents, securely tied on their hats, and "methodically began to pack their trunks," continuing to do so even when the regimental wagonmaster yelled at them "to run for their lives."[11]

By the time the two women had finished packing, they found the camp deserted. Clutching their baggage, they made their way on foot for several miles until they came across an astonished lieutenant who screamed, "For God's sake, run for the river. The Rebels are coming." Shells were now exploding about them; the road to the river had been churned into a soggy mess from horses' hooves, wagons, gun caissons, and weary men. Just before reaching the river, Belle and Mrs. N. found themselves surrounded by ambulances carrying men to an open-air dressing station. They put down their belongings, took off their bonnets, and set to work dressing wounds.[12]

As in the Revolutionary War, enlisted wives also accompanied and sometimes fought beside their husbands. Stocky, black-haired Kady Brownell (wife of Sergeant Robert Brownell) is said to have gone into action with the First Rhode Island Infantry at the First Battle of Bull Run. Carrying the company standard, and with shells falling all around her, "She stood with her flag out in the open to guide the men who were struggling through underbrush and trees, back to their line."[13] When the Union line broke, apparently Kady and a few troops continued to stand their ground until a retreating Pennsylvania trooper, realizing she was a woman, called, "Come, sis, there's no use to stay here just to be killed—let's get into the woods."[14] (Not all records agree on Kady's exploits; some indicate the battlesite was New Bern instead of Bull Run. Also, a February 2, 1866, letter from Job Arnold, a private in the regiment with Mrs. Brownell's husband, states he believes there is no foundation to "the great many stories of wonderful exploits performed during that campaign [Bull Run] by Mrs. Brownell.")[15]

Another wife, Bridget Divers, who was known as "Irish Bridget," joined her husband in the First Michigan Cavalry where she served as a nurse. She remained with the army for many years, and eventually fought Indians on the frontier as a regimental laundress.[16]

Southern women also fought along with their husbands. Mrs. Elizabeth Cardwell went on government transport with her husband, Private Patrick Cardwell of Virginia, a former Confederate who left with the First U.S. Volunteer Regiment. Then there was Mrs. Malinda Blalock of North Carolina, who posed as her husband's brother and enlisted, or Mrs. Amy Clarke, "who enlisted with her husband and continued in the service after he was killed at Shiloh. Not until she was wounded a second time and captured by the Federals was her sex detected."[17]

Of course, some accounts of wives at war had a lighter side. It was noted that Mrs. Dorsey Pender visited her husband, the general, three times—and each time she left pregnant.[18] Once when General George Meade's wife Margaret visited him in Virginia, he decided to remain with her in City Point instead of returning to camp. That night Confederate General Robert E. Lee mounted a surprise attack against Meade's troops. The attack was quickly repulsed, but Meade had always dreaded being absent from his post during an enemy attack. He sent a message to Margaret stating, "I am very glad you came, [but] I do expect to be pitched into by the *Tribune* for sleeping with you when Lee attacked our lines."[19]

There were also numerous accounts of gaiety: parties, formal balls, and some lush entertaining. Septima Levy Collins of Charleston, who married Union Army Captain Charles Henry Collins, recalled the interval of 1863-1864, in camp on the Potomac, as an unthinking time with extravagant balls and feasts. Laura Stratton Birney, a Philadelphia bride, was so enthusiastic she began her letters, "Three Cheers for Camp Life." And Princess Salms-Salms, wife of Prussian Prince Felix, who served with the Union Army, enjoyed a "large carpeted hospital tent . . . furnished with a damask-upholstered sofa and a large bedstead with a red and white silk canopy, and a smaller tent sheltered their kitchen and accommodations for her maid."[20]

Since many encampments were very close to towns, it was a fairly common practice for many wives to plan day-long visits to husbands. Sometimes men provided privacy by concealing the interior of their tents with garlands of pine, cedar, or holly fastened to a temporary framework. Secluded in this cool comfort

> wives of officers, in their brief visits to the front, find a most pleasant abiding place, from which they return with reluctance to city homes. An indescribable charm surrounds such life. . . . Its recollections are treasured among the happiest memories of the field, and many a country woman will wear a brighter dress for the lessons of adornment army life has taught.[21]

HELP OR HINDRANCE?

Whether or not they were welcome in the camps seems not to have deterred the women. Also, since battles were fought in and around populated areas, it was not uncommon for civilians—men, women, and children—to visit campsites on an almost daily basis and to observe battles. This does not mean that the accompanying wives did not have their critics. Mary Chesnut was not kind to her sister campfollowers and indicated in her diary that the war effort was not always uppermost in the minds of all wives. Writing about some she had encountered in Richmond, she complains, "They are so busy playing *court* here they forget the war *altogether*—these women!"[22]

Some husbands replied to wives' requests to visit them by indicating that "I should be as glad 2 [sic] see you as anybody would 2 see their wife." However, they discouraged the wives from joining them, indicating that camps were "not a fit place for any woman, for there is all kinds of talk, songs and everything not good for them to hear."[23]

Again, wives who followed found their welfare was not the prime consideration of the army. If the soldiers had to move on, military conveyances would be used for the men, not the women.

Supplies were also a problem for both the North and the South, with Confederate food shortages especially serious due to the Northern blockade. Any small amount of food given to accompanying families meant a soldier might not eat.

Even more serious, by refusing to leave an endangered area, the women were often caught in the line of fire or in siege conditions such as those of Vicksburg and Petersburg, where they faced endless hardships and possible death. The women who refused to move out of Vicksburg when ordered to were said to have the "worst trials of any group of Confederate women in a city under siege. . . . for a period of several months, they found themselves bottled up in a city that was threatened with famine and whose entire area was within the range of attacking guns."[24]

While siege threatened some, others were vulnerable to capture. The wife of Confederate Brigadier General John B. Gordon, who kept a wagon specially fitted for sleeping and living and who always followed closely behind her husband's division, was almost captured at Winchester, Virginia, in 1864. The Confederate commander, Lieutenant General Jubal Early, who was against having wives tag along with their husbands, "expressed regret that the Yankees hadn't bagged her."[25]

Comments such as this didn't appear to bother the wives, however, and many officers' wives joined their husbands, particularly when the armies rested in winter quarters. Apparently, this was encouraged by some, especially the higher ranking officers when their own wives were involved. General Ulysses S. Grant was most eager to have his wife with him whenever possible and wrote that he wanted to see her and the children very much. He indicated when she should join him in Vicksburg in a June 9, 1863, letter:

Dear Julia:
. . . You may start down as soon as you receive this letter. If Vicksburg is not in our hands then you can remain on board the steamer at the landing with the prospect of my calling to see you occationally [sic].[26]

In fact, Lieutenant Colonel John A. Rawlins, who had been with Grant throughout most of his campaigns, felt Grant's wife Julia was an asset at headquarters because she was a restraining influence on Grant's tendency to drink too much. Julia was often in the field with the general for long periods, as were his children. Grant's thirteen-year-old son, Fred, stayed with him through a good part of the Vicksburg campaign.[27] A proud Grant wrote to Julia in a May 3, 1863 letter from Grand Gulf, Mississippi, that, "Fred is very well, enjoying himself hugely. He has heard balls whistle and is not moved in the slightest by it. He was very anxious to run the blockade of Grand Gulf."[28] If the general was concerned for the child's safety, it was not indicated in his letters to his wife.

General Benjamin Butler also insisted that his wife accompany him for she was "faithful, true, cool-headed, conscientious and conservative. . . ." Not only did Mrs. Butler make him a home but her advice could be trusted.[29] Even General Logan, who thought it improper for "nice ladies" to be with the army, changed his mind when he was wounded. He allowed his wife Mary to accompany him in the winter of 1862-1863.[30]

ANGELS OF MERCY

Organizations of many kinds generally materialize in times of strife, and the Civil War was no exception. Women who organized to aid the sick and wounded were the most welcome on or near the battlefields. In New York on April 29, 1861, Elizabeth Blackwell organized a meeting of several thousand women and founded the Women's Central Association for Relief (WCAR), whose initial purpose was to establish a nurses' training program. This became the nucleus of the United States Sanitary Commission (the "Sanitary") and utilized women as nurses in both volunteer and paid positions. In 1862, the Confederacy also provided for female nurses in army general hospitals.[31]

Whereas many of these nurses were single or widowed, wives of the soldiers also nursed in the hospitals and camps. Mrs. Anna

McMeens, wife of Surgeon D. McMeens of Sandusky, Ohio, accompanied her husband and was "one of the first women in Ohio who gave her individual time in a Military Hospital in administering to the necessities of the soldiers."[32]

Mrs. S. A. Martha Canfield, wife of Colonel Herman Canfield of the Seventy-first Ohio Regiment, accompanied her husband, "assisting and doing all the good she could for the soldiers until the battle of Shiloh where her husband was wounded and died a few hours after." After her husband's death Mrs. Canfield returned to the Army of the Mississippi and worked in the Memphis hospitals.[33]

Along with several other women, Mrs. Jerusha Small was on the battlefield at Shiloh with the Twelfth Iowa Regiment, helping tend her husband and other wounded troops. When the Confederates invaded the camp, she narrowly escaped capture. During subsequent days of nursing, she "contracted the disease known in those days as 'galloping consumption'" and was finally sent home to die.[34]

Perhaps the devotion of many of the wives who followed their husbands can best be expressed by the words of Jerusha Small. Critically ill and on her way home from the war, she was chastised by another female railroad passenger for risking her health at such a young age:

"No," replied Mrs. Small. "I feel I have acted right, for by going I think I have been the means of saving the life of my dear husband, which I consider of far more value than mine; because now he can help defend our country in its time of need."[35]

CHAPTER FOUR

THE CALICO CAMPFOLLOWER: 1865–1898

Alice Blackwell Baldwin hoisted her skirts and climbed into the waiting railroad car. With excitement wreathing her face, she waved goodbye to her parents and friends, goodbye to all that was familiar to her. She was leaving her comfortable home in Detroit to embark on an adventure as the new bride of a young army officer stationed at Fort Harker in central Kansas.

It was the winter of 1867. Her fine garments, stylish and appropriate for short trips in Eastern carriages, could not keep her warm enough in the unheated railroad car nor in the ox-drawn freight wagon which lurched over the frozen ruts in the road. She completed the final leg of the journey huddled in an army ambulance, but still her spirits were high. In spite of the harsh journey, she looked forward to her first set of quarters as the new Mrs. Baldwin. When at last the horses were reined to a halt, Alice clambered down searching the brilliant snowy landscape for signs of housing at Fort Harker (near the present town of Ellsworth). Her eyes scanned the bleak, snow-covered scene. All she saw was a flat countryside broken here and there with small, snow-covered mounds which she realized with dismay were barracks and officers' quarters. Entering one of the dugouts, she broke down in tears at the sight of her new home: one squalid room, one camp chair, two empty candle boxes and "a huge grimy stove, covered with rust and full of tobacco-stained ashes and chewed-out quids." The canvas ceiling sagged in the middle and, since it did not fully reach one wall, allowed various packrats and prairie mice to hang over the sides and survey their human roommates with interested, beady eyes.

As with so may other "good" military wives, it was reported that Alice Baldwin was up early the next morning to prepare her husband's breakfast. She stuck it out, moved another 1,000 miles west, and within the year gave birth to the first white baby born in Trinidad, Colorado Territory. This was only the beginning of Alice's life campfollowing as she continued to accompany her husband until he eventually retired from the service with the rank of major general.[1] When the Civil War ended, women like Alice Baldwin joined an expanding number of wives whose army husbands sought their futures on the frontier.

FRONTIER ARMY

After the surrender of Lee at Appomattox in 1865, the military had released the bulk of its soldiers to civilian life, again leaving a small regular army. By 1867, the actual strength of the regular army was only 38,540, including 10,000 soon-to-be-released volunteers. This left a limited number of soldiers to enforce law in the South, to patrol the Mexican border, and to hold in check great numbers of Sioux, Cheyennes, Arapahoes, Comanches, Nez Percés and many other smaller tribes. Although expansion to the West had not stopped during the Civil War, many frontier regulars had gone to fight in the East. Thus, "the work of the army between 1848 and 1861 had been practically undone, so far as safety in the great West was concerned."[2]

As before the war, promotions were slow and salaries for both enlisted and officers continued to be low. For those officers who had independent means, frontier life could be made somewhat more comfortable; for those who didn't, it could be a penurious existence that affected the whole family. Little in the way of education was available for children of frontier army families. Colonel Philippe Regis de Trobriand discussed in his journal officers in the Dakota Territory "who have no fortune" and were unable to provide an adequate education for their sons and daughters on army pay. "If they keep them with them in the military posts . . . any instruction is impossible . . . unless the mother can undertake it." He concluded that the whole family would be in poverty if the parents attempted to send the children *and* the wife back "to civilization" and to support two households on one officer's salary.[3] (It is doubtful that education for children of enlisted troops was of much concern during this era.)

During the years immediately following the Civil War, however, an interesting phenomenon occurred regarding the frontier military. Because of the limited size and relative isolation of this regular army, a sense of "family" developed. Soldiers' paths crossed many times as they shifted across the mountains and prairies from fort to fort and from territory to territory. The officer corps was small (estimates vary from 1,600 to 2,000 in any year). Men remained aware of the deeds of former comrades and the changes in each other's lives. Friendships—and animosities—were continually being severed and renewed. Although many of the men remained bachelors or left wives behind in the East, accompanying wives began to feel that they were also an important part of the army family in the West.

Our visions of "the frontier" (romanticized by films, television programs, and movies such as *Wagon Train, Fort Apache,* and *Little House on the Prairie*) inevitably include endless miles of prairie, parched in summer and snow-covered in winter; barren bluffs overlooking a windswept desert; menacing Indian war parties; days of isolation and grave markers near rough wagon-wheel ruts. To the pioneers, civilian or military, these visions were realities to be dealt with on a day-to-day basis. Consequently, women were warned against moving westward.

Nevertheless, countless young women married dashing officers and rugged troopers whom they accompanied in the romance, saga, and hard work of settling the American West. Life in the West might best be described as an exercise in isolation and boredom laced with moments of sorrow and fear. Survival required endless amounts of energy and resilience. As she had done before, the campfollower of the frontier made her mark in history and was many times a colorful and vibrant character.

TREKKING WEST

At the side of the frontier army men—in wagons or on horseback, by barge, stagecoach, and eventually train—were their apprehensive, excited, and spiritually tough women. Relocation was always a challenge for these women in the West. Eveline M. Alexander kept an upbeat, literate diary of her campfollowing in which day after day she records marching or riding from seven to twenty-two miles. Her tone suggests she made the best of quite stark living conditions.

> I have been several days in camp and take to it very kindly. I have everything arranged most comfortably for me. My tent is lined with blue army blankets, which not only protect it from dampness and make it much cooler on hot days, but subdues the light, which makes a distressing glare in the canvas tents. I have a buffalo skin for a carpet, and my bed is covered with the red blanket Fanny Rawles gave me.[4]

Through her words, an illustration of travel for frontier army wives is brought to life. For example, she describes a twenty-two-mile move to a new station:

> I presented quite a funny appearance. I was seated in a high rocking chair which was fastened by cleats to the bottom of the ambulance. Under my chair was my tin washbowl and pitcher . . . in front was my box of books (my traveling library). . . . Hanging from the top of the ambulance were two leather pockets, one of them containing my revolver, the other a field glass; a looking glass; my sewing basket; and a lantern also swayed to and fro. . . . A square of grass was cut first and then the tent pitched, and the odor of "new mown hay" was a great improvement on our late perfume,

"essence de cheval." I slept long and soundly, undisturbed by my natural enemies the flies.[5]

As with all military families, the Alexanders spent their lives moving from fort to fort. The experience of the family of the future General Douglas MacArthur is a perfect example. Douglas was born in 1880 in Little Rock, Arkansas, where his father was posted with the Thirteenth Infantry. (The building where they lived was like most military family quarters of the time: the second-floor rooms of an old arsenal which the Army no longer had an operational need for.) Soon after his birth, Doug and his mother Mary followed Captain MacArthur from Arkansas to Fort Wingate, New Mexico, where "facilities for families were bare . . . and life for Army wives was rugged."[6] Deep in her heart Mary probably longed for the old arsenal back in Arkansas. She was new at army life, and despite the beauty of the mountains surrounding Fort Wingate, the living conditions at Wingate must have been a shock.

The military, then as now, tested the flexibility of military families with sudden and uncomfortable moves. For the MacArthurs, this occurred in February 1884 when Captain MacArthur was ordered to Fort Selden, Texas. The MacArthurs traveled the 300-mile distance riding and walking through a succession of winter blizzards while all the time looking over their shoulders for the notorious Geronimo.[7]

Even chronic ill health did not deter Frances M. A. Roe from relocating with her husband, Lieutenant Fayette W. Roe, to forts in Colorado, Kansas, Montana, and Idaho. Well-educated at a private school in New York, Frances kept an explicit diary of her experiences, including a description of one move to Fort Benton in Montana Territory in 1878. She mentions her relief at being able to transfer to the relative comfort of an army ambulance after traveling several days by stagecoach, "one of the jerky bob-back-and-forth kind that pitches you off the seat every five minutes [where you] bump heads with the passenger sitting opposite you."[8]

Petite, dark-haired Elizabeth Bacon Custer, wife of General Custer, also traveled extensively over the West with her husband. The daughter of a Michigan judge, Libbie (like many other officers' wives) came from a fairly affluent background and had graduated from a female seminary. In her diaries, she paints a vivid picture of both the good and bad aspects of military moves. As an officer's wife, Mrs. Custer was usually accompanied in her travels by two servants. This was in stark contrast to her enlisted counterparts who could not afford such luxury and who many times worked as servants for the officer class.

THE ARISTOCRACY

As was the case during Revolutionary and Civil War times, accounts of the frontier military wives' experiences and lifestyle come mostly from the diaries and correspondence of officers' wives. No matter what her background or schooling, if a woman married an officer, she became a part of the aristocracy which the army created and reinforced. Frontier military wives tended to fall into three categories; officers' ladies, NCOs' wives, and enlisted mens' women (sometimes wives, sometimes not). This was not a formal class system and there were no written rules, but the barriers, while invisible, effectively sustained the military caste system.

Of course, the rigors, hardships, and hazardous conditions of the frontier tended to dilute the caste boundaries somewhat, for as one officer's wife put it: "There was the solitude of . . . mutual existence—just a handful of people, so to speak, afloat upon an uncharted sea of desolation . . . and the daily perils they faced together."9 All the women on an army post knew one another; sometimes the enlisted wives worked as maids in officers' homes; their children played with each other, attended school together (when there was one), and became friends. But there was no social interaction between the wives on Officers' Row and the enlisted wives and laundresses of Soapsuds Row, whom one source described as "good, honest, industrious wives, usually well on in years."[10]

Israel Gibbs, in a report sent to his newspaper from the frontier, noted:

> It is really curious to observe how well and how strictly the three classes of women in camp keep aloof from each other. The wives and daughters of colonels, captains and other officers constitute the first class. The rough cooks and washers who have their husbands along . . . form the second class. The third and last class is happily the smallest; here and there a female . . . truly wife-like in their tented seclusion, but lacking that great and only voucher of respectability for females in camp—the marriage tie.[11]

Although social contact between officer and enlisted wives was severely limited, it had become the custom of the service that a soldier's wife could always come to the commander's wife for counsel and advice on problems. It was also the custom that the officer's wife would do her utmost to aid the soldier's wife.[12] Still, each wife knew and maintained her position in the hierarchy.

HOME, SWEET HOME

While living conditions were difficult for all wives, they were always better for the officers' wives. Mention is frequently made in diaries and letters of domestic help in the officers' homes. One form of servant available at the frontier garrisons was the "striker," an enlisted man who would work for an officer during his off-duty hours. Martha Summerhayes vowed that she "could not have survived her life on the frontier without the faithful ministrations" of striker Charles Bowen.[13] Elizabeth Custer wrote that she had excellent servants and that "domestic care sat very lightly on me." Custer did not like to have Elizabeth in the kitchen and asked her to leave the domestic chores to the servants.[14]

Housing varied from fort to fort, but was usually better for the officers' families, although this is difficult to believe judging from some of the descriptions given. When the MacArthurs arrived at Fort Wingate, Arizona, Mary MacArthur found

> The cramped quarters offered little privacy, and few were the luxuries that women love and find so necessary to their morale. The primitive adobe buildings, the worn pieces of furniture, the patched dresses, the dust from the drill ground which crept into every nook of the quarters—such depressing sights must have made her feel she was trapped at the far edge of nowhere.[15]

Elizabeth Custer tells of a friend accompanying her husband, Colonel Frederick Benteen, on detached duty to an isolated part of Dakota Territory. To keep the cold from coming through the floor, the Benteens stuffed strips of gunny sacking in the cracks. Since walls of their hut were unplastered, the enterprising Mrs. Benteen papered each wall with pages from the *Army and Navy Journal* and decorated the printed pages with illustrations from *Harper's Weekly*.[16]

Describing her own quarters in Kansas, Mrs. Custer indicates that the rooms were small and nearly bare of furniture. (It seems that even the general's furniture was not what would be expected for a commanding officer's quarters.) Using ingenuity, she and some of the other wives on the post made lounges from boards covered with cretonne or calico-covered pillows stuffed with hay. Usually the Custers tried to keep one carpet intact for the parlor, but in their bedroom the carpet consisted of four gray government blankets which had been bought at a sale of condemned goods and which Elizabeth had darned, sewed together, and spread in the center of the floor.[17] (Of course, even if a family could afford luxuries, most times they were not readily available.)

A dining room floor of sand from which little white toadstools grew greeted the Roes when they reached their quarters at Camp Supply, Indian Territory, in 1872. The logs in their home were of cottonwood, "and have the bark on, and the army of bugs that hide underneath the bark during the day and march upon us at night is to be dreaded about as much as a whole tribe of Indians!"[18] Later they were moved into a much nicer home of cedar logs, but their kitchen was located across the yard and had been a chicken coop.[19]

If post conditions were not ideal for the officers' wives, they were even worse for the wives of the lower ranks. Most of them were in camp as laundresses and lived in Sudsville "east of the sewer outlet . . . a collection of huts, old tents, picket houses and dugouts . . . an air of squalor and dirt about the locality . . . together with troops of shock-headed children, prowling curs and scavenging chickens."[20]

Sometimes enlisted quarters were small cabins out beyond the company barracks; at other times, as at Fort Gibson in 1867, no quarters were available and both troops and laundresses had to live in tents.[21] At Fort Sill, Oklahoma, in 1870, the married soldiers and their laundress wives were also forced to live in tents. (However, by 1874, Fort Sill had abolished Sudsville and enlisted families were finally quartered in stone houses west of the barracks).[22] As late as 1875, at Fort Dodge, Kansas, married soldiers were in dugouts or sod buildings along the river bank. At Camp McDowell in Arizona, enlisted families lived in tumbledown adobe huts characterized by the post surgeon as "unfit to live in."[23]

Even if enlisted housing was available, most times it was cramped, dreary, and inadequately heated or ventilated. In December 1889, at Fort Robinson, Nebraska, the surgeon mentions a dwelling "occupied by a corporal, his wife and child [consisting] of a single room, built of waste lumber about 12 feet square and with no window or other opening except the door . . . to stand open most of the time and admits light and dust in equal abundance."[24]

After the Civil War many black soldiers remained in the army or enlisted and were on the frontier in black cavalry troops known as "buffalo soldiers." Like the white wives, black wives accompanied their husbands to the West and coped with whatever housing was available. A July 1891 report by Fort Robinson's assistant surgeon, Captain George W. Adair, enumerates the women and children and tells of their housing by racial characteristics:

> an abandoned log barrack whose squad room is used as a Quartermasters' store room, has the orderly room, kitchen, and mess-room, together with enclosed portions of the old porch, occupied by soldiers' families. Fifteen small rooms contain eight soldiers wives—all colored—and ten children. . . . Another abandoned barrack . . . in like manner shelters four married women—three colored and one white—and six colored children, and one adult male civilian colored.[25]

Naturally, some forts had better housing than others. Apparently excellent housing (for that time) was available for officers at Fort Towson, Arkansas, and one army general felt construction "should have been foremost for defense instead of luxurious officers' quarters." Built of pine logs hewn on two sides, the quarters each contained four rooms and a kitchen with a basement under half of the building. Walls were whitewashed and all rooms had ceilings.[26]

Frances Roe's quarters at Fort Ellis, Montana Territory, were much improved in 1879 over her earlier ones at Camp Supply: "Our houses are really very warm—the thick logs are plastered inside and papered, every window has a storm sash and every room a double floor, and our big stoves can burn immense logs."[27]

Even enlisted quarters were not always substandard. Laundress Rachel Loback who married Henry F. Brown of F Company, Fourth Infantry in 1874 and followed him to the Red Cloud Agency (Nebraska), was one of the few enlisted wives to keep a diary. Although probably the exception to the rule, she records that they were housed in a log cabin and she had an Indian woman to help with the laundry and household chores. She also comments that many of the ladies wore red flannels to help ward off the cold.[28]

Old frame shanties and stone buildings occupied by married enlisted at Fort Lyon, Colorado Territory, were considered to be exceptionally good quarters compared to those at some posts. At Jefferson Barracks near St. Louis, the post surgeon felt that quarters for the laundresses and married soldiers were better than he had seen at any other post.[29]

Of course, attitude may have played a big part in how a wife coped with frontier living, but it must have been difficult to see the bright side after monotonous months in bleak, windswept areas. Elizabeth Custer lamented the lack of flowers to brighten her quarter's drab interior. Sometimes in the shade of cottonwood trees clematis could be found, and then garlands draped barren rooms. Wildflowers sprang up across the prairies but were soon scorched by the summer sun. One time a friend gave Elizabeth some pressed ferns, and she pasted these on the windows in an attempt to create a feeling of cool nooks in a leafy forest. She considered the sunbaked plains to be a "flowerless land . . . like the desert of Sahara," and longed for the wild daisies and ferns of the East. Occasionally there would be some family who enlivened their dwelling with paintings. "Someone who painted in oils or water colors would triumph over the obstacles of our life, and their walls were our envy."[30]

Unlike Elizabeth Custer, Emily Fitzgerald McCorkle, wife of Dr. Jenkins (John) A. Fitzgerald, did not seem to be bothered by the starkness of the plains. Writing to her mother on May 26, 1876, Emily described the area surrounding Fort Lapwai, Idaho Territory, as "rich prairie land with such pretty wild flowers and such herds of fat sheep and cows."[31] Margaret Irvin Carrington commented on the "wild tulip, larkspur, sweet pea, convolvulus . . . duly pressed for future care and admiration."[32]

At Fort Washakie, in central Wyoming, Caroline Frey Winne wrote fifty-seven letters and cards to her father and brother back in Palatine Bridge, New York. Like Elizabeth Custer she would learn that most of the year the scenery would consist of sagebrush and prickly pear, but in spring of 1879, she could write:

> This post is pleasantly located right on the bank of little Wind River and in full view of the snow covered mountains on one side. The parade is green and small trees are growing in the post—along the bank of the river are quite large trees.[33]

Elizabeth Helmick was also quite impressed by the "snow-covered mountains which seemed so near the frosted pines sparkling in the sunshine," as she traveled by sleigh in 1890 to Fort Spokane, Washington, with her young lieutenant husband.[34]

Margaret Carrington, particularly, seemed to have a positive attitude toward the continuing problems of frontier domestic life.

> The snapping of a tent-pole at midnight under three feet of snow; the blaze of the canvas, as the ambitious fire commissions the red-hot pipe to unroof your earthly tabernacle, at no small risk to bedding and trunks; the pretty little drifts that gracefully slip through the closely drawn entrance and sprinkle your bed, your furniture and your wardrobe, all afford change and excitement . . . are incentives to new branches of industry and skill.[35]

Perhaps for many wives the sense of adventure and excitement enabled them to deal with the very real dangers of frontier existence.

DISEASE AND DANGER

Regardless of how a wife might feel about the quality of her quarters or the frontier in general, disease was an ever-present threat. Shortly after the Civil War, Colonel Charles Augustus Ropes Dimon, in command of a replacement troop for Fort Rice, wrote in his diary of the trek through Dakota Territory in the hail, rain, and raw winds to reach the fort. George H. W. Herrick, the command's doctor, who had taken the position at Fort Rice because of the opportunities for extensive practice, earlier had made the journey across the territory with his wife. She died the day Dimon's troops reached the fort. A poem written about Mrs. Herrick's death comments upon death in Dakota and likens the trackless western plains to "a limitless waste of ocean."[36]

Along with the troops, wives contracted dysentery, scurvy, cholera, measles, diphtheria, and a host of other illnesses. Pregnancy and childbirth were hard on both woman and newborn: miscarriages were frequent and convalescence many times was lengthy.[37]

Sanitary conditions were generally deplorable, and indoor plumbing did not exist. When Elizabeth Custer's cook needed to get rid of kitchen waste water, she merely opened the door and flung the contents of the dishpan or garbage bucket to one side.[38] Not only did this make for an unsightly yard, but it provided a breeding ground for germs.

In addition to illness, Indian raids were always a frightening possibility. Frances Roe writes of an incident at Camp Supply in 1872:

Night before last the post was actually attacked by Indians! It was about one o'clock when the entire garrison was awakened by rifle shots and cries of "Indians! Indians!" There was pandemonium at once.[39]

Roe, with a revolver in her hand, and a Mrs. Hunt huddled on the steps at the front door for several hours, hoping to protect themselves and Hunt's three small children. Just before dawn they learned that a cavalry troop had been patrolling around the post and they were apparently in little danger.[40]

In her diary Margaret Carrington mentions problems with the Indians several times. At Fort Reno, Montana, the sutler's horses and mules were stolen. Warnings were posted at the sutler's store warning emigrants of how "to deal with or not deal with the Indians." Over a period of only two months, she recounts dozens

of visits, thefts, and deaths involving Indians and military men
or settlers.[41]

Many times when traveling through hostile territory, wives
were instructed to lie on the floor of the wagons to escape
detection by Indians. Often a white woman was captured, put
through a gang rape and then, to use an Indian phrase, "thrown
away" on the plains. Elizabeth Custer wrote of one such woman
who straggled into camp "quite mad and couldn't remember who
she was."[42]

Occasionally drastic measures were necessary during Indian
attacks. At a siege of Fort Phil Kearney in Nebraska, the fort
commander assembled all the women and children in the powder
magazine and gave orders to the first sergeant to fire it if the
Indians breeched the fort walls. At Fort Buford in the Dakotas in
1867, the commanding officer and 80 men held off 3,000 Indians
for two days. When it appeared that the garrison would soon be
overpowered, the commander shot his wife (the only woman on
the post) and himself.[43]

In addition to the women's fear of Indian attack, there was
always the fear that husbands might not return from scouting
parties or routine patrols. From Fort Lapwai, Idaho Territory, in
August 1877, Emily McCorkle awaited the return of her physician
husband, who was with troops fighting the Nez Percé Indians in
Montana. Expressing her anxiety, she wrote to her mother:

> Indeed, I have never been so unhappy in my life. . . . This
> uncertainty of everything in the future, and this not knowing
> or hearing anything is the hardest thing to bear. . . . I have
> heard nothing from Doctor himself for almost a month. . . .
> I am very anxious and worried about my dear husband. . . .
> I wish all this war was over and John home again.[44]

For Frances Courtney Grummond, the fear of her husband not
returning from a military engagement became a reality. On
December 21, 1866, Frances, who was several months pregnant
with her first child, watched her young husband, Lieutenant

George Grummond, accompany Captain William J. Fetterman and forty-six soldiers in pursuit of Indians who had attacked a wood train bound for Fort Phil Kearney. Shots from the ensuing fight could be heard at the fort. Soon the word came back—there were no survivors of what came to be known as the "Fetterman Massacre." Throughout the four days before Christmas, Frances watched men dig graves in the frozen ground. "I knew that my husband's coffin was being made, and the sound of hammers and the grating of saws was torture." (Frances Grummond carried her husband's remains home to Tennessee in March 1867, where a few weeks later their son was born.)[45]

THE BRIGHTER SIDE

Most army wives did not dwell on the hardships and dangers of frontier living. For both the officer and enlisted wives, spots of brightness existed on the prairie as they had in the forts of the Northeast, the Great Lakes, and the Appalachians. Balls were held frequently, and at the larger garrisons wives arranged picnics, parties and amateur theatricals. Visiting dignitaries were given fancy dinners, although many of these were given on borrowed finery. Katherine Gibson recalled a party at Fort Lincoln, Nebraska, where a long table was set up on sawhorses, with a rubber bucket of wildflowers marking each joint. "Handerchiefs served to cover bare planks in lieu of doilies, which gave something of a festive touch, the men gallantly declaring the effect to be ravishing."[46]

Elizabeth Custer belonged to a reading club organized by one wife at Fort Lincoln. Each week the ladies met to discuss new books which had been sent for from the East. Mrs. Custer also described in great detail the preparations for the balls given by each company during the winter at Fort Lincoln. Bunks were removed from the barracks, which were then decorated with flags. Chandeliers were carved and filled with candles; huge logs were placed in the fireplaces. In low neck and short sleeves, the ladies' toilets [sic] "were something marvelous in construction."

Refreshments many times consisted of "a great dish of potato salad. It was always well flavored with the onion, as rare out there . . . as pomegranates are in New York." Sometimes there was cake, a great luxury.[47]

Elizabeth and Eli Helmick considered riding to be one of their "greatest pleasures" while at Fort Spokane. Often they hunted mountain grouse or quail. Elizabeth also gave dinners and dances, and her card parties to play whist, 500, euchre, Napoleon, and poker were well attended by the officers and their ladies. In addition, tennis was popular and "croquet was played during the long summer evenings." Another form of amusement at the fort was "walking on the board walk extending along the front of officers quarters . . . and constituted the lighter exercise for both officers and ladies."[48]

At Fort Union, New Mexico, troops were welcomed back with a series of hops, Frances Boyd recalls:

We had only to notify the quartermaster that a hop was to be given, when our barren hallway would immediately be transferred into a beautiful ballroom, with canvas stretched tightly over the floor, flags decorating the sides, and ceiling so charmingly draped as to make us feel doubly patriotic.[49]

Christmas was always anticipated with eagerness, according to Frances Roe. It was customary for army wives to visit "along the line Christmas morning . . . giving each other pleasant greetings" while they enjoyed the gifts each had received. Then the married women usually took homemade candy or cakes to the bachelor officers' quarters. After chapel services the company officers and wives went to the barracks to "see the mens' dinner tables," but not to dine with them. (In 1871, dinner for the enlisted men at Fort Lyon, Colorado Territory, consisted of buffalo, antelope, boiled ham, vegetables, pickles, pies, and the large plum cakes which officers' wives customarily sent to the men in their husbands' companies.)[50]

For those women in California and the Southwest, contact with the Hispanics brought a great deal of interest. Some learned to speak Spanish and to prepare Mexican food. Although some army wives were initially shocked by the "immodest" dress of the Mexican women, they soon came to appreciate the adaptation of dress to the climate. A few wives overcame their fear of Indians enough to visit Indian camps and even to entertain Indian women in their homes. As the soldiers' wives observed the Indian customs, many of their preconceptions about the Indians as a stolid, humorless, stupid, dangerous people vanished.[51] This contact with the Hispanics and the Indians not only provided diversion from the boredom of camplife for the army wives, it also broadened their knowledge of different cultures and helped them learn to cope with new situations.

HELPMATES OR HANDICAPS?

With so many more wives accompanying their husbands to western stations in the latter half of the nineteenth century, one might assume that their presence was no longer an issue for debate. However this was not the case. Duane Merritt Greene, who had been an officer before leaving the army, thought the two worst influences around an army post were whiskey and officers' wives. Greene felt the ladies monopolized the time of their husbands and bachelor officers and that discipline was most lacking at posts where there were a great number of wives. One enlisted man viewed officers' wives as "painted dolls" who did not belong on the frontier posts as they had no legal status. He felt the post laundresses were the only real ladies of the post.[52]

Another source, however, indicates that while the laundresses usually did their work well, they were often a source of trouble. "There are cases on record . . . when the officer of the day had to be sent to Sudsville to break up arguments among the laundry 'spikes' which surpassed the cigarette-factory scene from Carmen."[53] At Fort Concho, Texas, a black laundress was dismissed for theft and general impudence while three white laundresses were expelled for drunkenness, lewdness, and worthlessness.[54]

The status of officers' wives was ambiguous. Many wrote in their memoirs that the War Department took no notice of them in army regulations and that they had the status of "campfollowers." On the other hand, they complained, laundresses and servants (also campfollowers) had legal standing in army regulations. However, this was not a true picture. While in military law wives were campfollowers because they were civilians, regulations occasionally made reference to officers' families and, although not providing for them, at least recognized their existence. Military men were not prohibited from marrying (although they were not encouraged to do so), but no provisions were made in Washington for the men to take their wives westward.[55]

Like many of the officers, General James Parker found the companionship of his wife a great solace in the dreary routine of frontier army life. Although his wife had come from luxurious surroundings, at military posts she "faced the hardships of the frontier without a murmur . . . was proud of doing her part to serve our country. . . . Like a true soldier, she soon came to love the regiment, the troops." Mrs. Parker developed into an expert horsewoman and spent many hours exploring the plains with the general. For a few hours each day she helped ease his cares. "With her, life was a poem."[56]

Naturally, the wives thought they made a great contribution to the welfare and morale of their men. One wife, journeying with the Third Infantry into Montana in 1877, wrote:

The officers are singing and whistling, and we can often hear from the distance the boisterous laughter of the men. . . . We know, if the world does not, that the part we are to take on this march is most important. We will see that the tents are made comfortable and cheerful at every camp; that the little dinner after the weary march, the early breakfast, and the cold luncheon are each and all as dainty as the camp cooking will permit.[57]

She continues that while some envious old bachelor officer may have labeled them "campfollowers," the women did not mind, for they knew they brought comfort and cheer, and most importantly, "we have not been left behind."[58]

Another woman felt that the army wives were most needed on the marches and at dreary camps, like Camp Supply, Indian Territory, with its bleak log and mud huts. She could be, this wife thought, a comforting and restraining influence over the entire garrison.[59]

Elizabeth Custer also felt that the presence of wives on army posts was beneficial. She did question that "with all the value that is set on the presence of the women of an officer's family at the frontier posts" why army regulations made no provision for them. She felt that the army was so meticulous in some details, even giving the number of hours that bean soup should boil, that it should at least devote a paragraph to the officer's wife.[60]

On December 20, 1889, the assistant surgeon at Fort Robinson, Nebraska, wrote a lengthy letter against the expulsion of families from military reservations, which he felt

> would cause much hardship and suffering to the women and children, and discontent among their husbands. . . . Marriage undoubtedly increases the steadiness and reliability of the soldier, as it does in the case of other men. . . . It is a very rare occurrence for a married man to desert. . . . The married soldier loses fewer days from sickness than his single comrade.[61]

The surgeon went on to recommend that it would "be much better to give them [the women and children] official recognition under certain conditions and restrictions . . . and to furnish them with proper quarters."[62]

Regardless of arguments for or against the campfollower or her lack of official status, the army wife did persevere. From the beginning of the great westward expansion until the frontier was considered conquered at the end of the nineteenth century, she cared for her husband, gave birth to her children, and maintained the military family lifestyle in countless dugouts and mud huts at long-forgotten garrisons. Having conquered one frontier, she turned her eyes to other farflung posts and packed her bags for foreign assignments.

CHAPTER FIVE

OVER THE WAVES

Through the waves of heat shimmering on the steel deck of an army troop ship, Elizabeth Helmick first glimpsed the lush Philippine Islands she would call home for the next two years.[1] The year was 1901, and she was already a seasoned army wife who always did her utmost to accompany her husband—even to places wives of that time normally did not go. Married in 1888 to Eli A. Helmick, a young West Point graduate, she was at a western outpost for the Indian uprisings of 1890 and then at Havana and Santiago during the army occupation of Cuba in 1898. For a stretch of some months she would be the only white woman accompanying United States troops to a remote outpost in the Philippines.

The trip to the Philippines was not without mishap. First she waited six weeks, "in camp" in San Francisco with two small children for transport to the Philippines. Once on board, an epidemic of smallpox broke out. Then her children caught the measles and were quarantined for twenty-eight days.

"Just one of the vicissitudes of army life," she would say. To Elizabeth, civilian life would have been dull, and her life as an army wife had taught her much. "You see we learn what is essential. We learn to enjoy life as those who are bound by conventions never learn." Resilience and humor seemed hallmarks of this remarkable woman. When separated from her husband, her letters were filled with longing to be with him interspersed with practical concerns of daily life. Other than terrible loneliness, she complained of little. Even when their young daughter died in Rhode Island, thousands of miles away from them, she mourned in silence. In spite of all she endured, life for Elizabeth was an adventure in which she remembered the good things and suffered the hurts privately.

The Helmicks were in the forefront of what would become known as "the American military family overseas." Near the end of the nineteenth century, the United States, although officially following a policy of isolationism, gradually became involved in economic expansion and political alliances abroad. To protect both American investment abroad and territories taken by the United States through war, treaty, or purchase, the navy and army left their home bases and became part of American expansionism. The army wife packed up her home and took to the sea.

Even as it approached the twentieth century, the military still had not established an official policy regarding accompanying wives and children. Although the numbers of wives campfollowing were increasing, the military ignored them as much as possible. Their transportation, quarters, rations, medical care, and protection from hostile forces were still provided by the husband who was foolish enough to take on this responsibility. Families journeyed overseas at their own risk.

ALASKA

The Alaska Territory (purchased from Russia in 1867) was one of the first overseas postings where wives had an opportunity to broaden their horizons. Although records from this period do not give specific numbers for accompanying wives, the mention of spouses from time to time shows that the military wife was determined to experience this new adventure.

As early as 1874, Emily Fitzgerald McCorkle, wife of an army doctor, wrote extensively to her mother about their arrival in Sitka and the fact that everyone came down to the wharf to meet them, "ladies and all." Her newsy letters describe their quarters as "the nicest" and cover practically every detail from the carpet brought from Portland to the green ruffled window curtains and ash furniture. In addition, as had become a common practice for many officers' families, the McCorkles had a live-in maid and a black cook, leaving Emily "with nothing to do." Life was not totally free from stress, however, as Emily added, "I told you we had been nearly devoured by fleas, didn't I?"[2]

Mrs. Barendina Gardener Chambers recalled in a series of sketches her childhood in Alaska with her mother and father (Colonel Cornelius Gardener). Particularly moving is her account of the death in childbirth of Kathleen, the wife of the regimental bandleader.

> So my mother, the colonel's wife, gathered together the ladies of the garrison, who brought out their summer bonnets to take from them whatever gay and colorful floral decorations were suitable. Quickly and sadly, they made as best they could a bright wreath of colored blossoms . . . laid it in the slim coffin of the pretty young lass.[3]

Elizabeth Helmick also was to make the Alaskan journey, but at a later time. In letters home to her mother, Elizabeth gave a detailed picture of life at the edge of a glacier. In April 1907, she wrote that she passed a very trying two weeks as the wind came off the mountainside

> over the great Valdez glacier, and surging between two steep mountains rushes down the valley across the bay and reaches us in the strength of its fury, cold, cutting and terrible. Our great house is on the top of a small hill right in the path of the wind, and day and night the great structure would tremble and shake, and we were obliged to abandon the use of the rooms facing the glacier as it was impossible to warm them.

In a February 1986, interview, the Helmicks' daughter, Florence Pinkerton, recalled how they were caught by "falling bricks" and had to give up the great house with its magnificent view when a major—who outranked her captain father—was transferred from Hawaii to command Fort Liscum. Mrs. Helmick stoically accepted the change in living quarters, writing:

> This will turn us out of our lovely large house and put us in one of the cottages along the line. I part with my magnificent view with great sadness, but otherwise, without a servant, it will be a good thing for me, and besides having another in command will transfer the necessity of entertaining to another, and I will not get so worn out in a smaller house.

Elizabeth's complaint about "the necessity of entertaining" would be echoed down through the years by other officers' wives, especially those whose husbands were post commanders. Whereas entertaining brightened the routine at many a dreary post and was unofficially considered a "necessity" in the officer ranks, many times it was a financial hardship, as the military did not pay for it. "Prices are simply prohibitive," Elizabeth mentioned, and on one occasion when the bishop was coming to lunch found that she had only a little bacon in the house. She made do by serving plain bouillon with crisp crackers as her first course followed by baked potatoes, a little vegetable salad, baking powder biscuits made with butter, and the bacon. Using all her "drawn and embroidered doilies" and serving the dishes on a highly polished table, she was able to put together a presentable meal.

CUBA

Long before her sojourn in Alaska, Elizabeth had followed her husband to Cuba—in 1898, shortly after the Spanish–American War. Eli Helmick wrote of his efforts to locate suitable quarters in Havana for his family. Apparently the first house he found was not satisfactory for he returned home one day only to discover that Elizabeth had moved the family to another, larger residence.

Maude "Tiss" Palmer arrived in Cuba in 1900 to find her husband, Lieutenant John M. Palmer, had obtained living quarters in an old Spanish mansion in Puerto Principe. Her ankles were constantly bitten by fleas that lived in the brick floors, but her greatest surprise was the "buxom black cook preparing breakfast with a big cigar in her mouth." Fleas and cigar-smoking cooks aside, the Palmers at least had their privacy in the roomy old mansion. A few weeks later they would be moved to the regimental camp and housed with several other officers' families in two hospital tents, with only an awning separating the quarters.[4]

However, by 1907, when James Parker was sent to take command of the army regiment in Pinar del Rio, it appears that comfortable quarters were more plentiful. The Parkers lived in a one-story house with "a spacious veranda in front and a patio in the rear, containing the cook house, offices, etc." The house had tile floors, and the Parkers had one servant who "performed the various duties of cook, housemaid and laundryman."[5]

Lieutenant Colonel Robert L. Bullard found while visiting the Twenty-Eighth Infantry (part of the Army of Cuban Pacification sent to Cuba by the United States because of the Cuban Civil War of 1906) "that most of the officers had brought their families to Cuba and were thoroughly enjoying their tropical winter. . . ." Unfortunately, Bullard's wife Rose and his two young children did not fair as well. Shortly after arriving in Havana, they became seriously ill and were forced to return to the states after only two weeks.[6]

THE PHILIPPINES

For Elizabeth Helmick, the first of many adventures in the Philippines happened when her husband was among the 150 men ordered to occupy the island of Paragua. As the only woman on ship with the troops, she heard the insurrectionists of Paragua vow to die before they would surrender. At the sight of the armed men, Elizabeth took her children below deck to wait out the fight. It never took place. Within an hour the American commander

General Kobbe, sent her the rebels' white sheet of surrender,
letting her know all was well. The family disembarked and for
two months stayed on the island in a magnificent old Spanish
house, seeing not another white face other than the troops and
having no communication with the outside. She then accompanied
her husband and his troops to Catabato, arriving July 30, 1902.
Their quarters were a large, rambling convent roofed in tin, with
rooms high off the ground and facing the river. In a letter to her
mother, Elizabeth wrote:

> The charm of the house is its proximity to the river, which is
> very pretty and constantly filled with boats laden with pictur-
> esque Moros, Filipinos, Chinas [sic] etc. All the windows are
> very wide, having . . . bamboo awnings and sliding, wooden
> shutters. When all are open it is like being on a broad piazza.

It was in this house that Elizabeth had to deal not only with an
earthquake soon after arriving, but with a betel-chewing
princessa who claimed everything she saw as hers, and a "ghost."
   "We had been in Catabato less than a month when we had our
first . . . experience with an earthquake," wrote Eli in his journal. He and Elizabeth were playing cards with another couple,
when a shout of "earthquake" made him look up.

> I saw the stone wall of the house in front of me opening and
> closing along the sides of a heavy wooden upright which
> supported the roof beams. Everyone made a dash for the
> ground floor. [Elizabeth] was lighter and more active than
> most women of her age. She was the first one down the
> stairs. . . . She chided me for helping Mrs. Reid and not her.

It took ingenuity to outwit the reigning *princessa* of Catabato.
Florence Pinkerton recalled:

> The *Princessa* chewed betel juice and spat on Mother's
> chairs. . . . Everything she saw, she wanted. Mother would

have to say, "It is yours." She got tired of this. Mary Ruth, our nanny, came up with a way to fool the *Princessa* by putting away everything Mother liked and leaving out things she didn't want anymore.

Mrs. Pinkerton also remembered the incident of the ghost who went thump in the night—of course, when her father was not at home. When he returned he investigated the scary noises ". . . which is humourous now but which caused us a number of sleepless nights then . . ." only to discover their ghost was nothing more than a large rat that had dragged the remains of their dinner hambone thumping down the stairs.

Like Elizabeth Helmick, Tiss Palmer had an interesting journey to the Philippines. Reaching Manila after a lengthy sea voyage, she then journeyed nine days by steamer to a village called Iligan where her husband met her. From there it was another day's journey by dougherty wagon to Marahui, which Palmer labeled "the wilds of Moroland."[7]

Tiss's housing in Marahui was acceptable but primitive. Naturally, there was no hot water and the Palmers' shower consisted of a ten-gallon can overhead and a string used to tip the can and pour out water. (John was quite pleased with his invention for bathing, but Tiss was not impressed.) However, there was adequate garden space and Tiss soon provided quantities of vegetables for the dinner table, including delicacies such as American green peas and lima beans. Later the family moved into a thatch house at nearby Camp Keithly where, when "the rain fell, the thatch leaked, so we had to place umbrellas over our pillows."[8]

As in earlier times, some situations were dangerous or cause for sorrow. Eda Blankart Funston, who had joined her husband Colonel (later Major General) Frederick Funston in the Philippines in 1899, lived off-base in Manila. Philippine patriots, upon learning that the United States was going to take over control of their land from Spain, took up arms to fight for freedom. The Funstons, along with other nearby military families, were roused from their beds in the middle of the night, and the wives were

told to go to the barracks for safety. Although some of the wives
were quite fearful, Eda Funston

> calmly packed my toothbrush, towels, and other necessities;
> the other ladies marveled that I should think of such things
> at such a time. . . . I shall never forget that walk to the
> barracks. Every step seemed to add a century to my life, the
> guns on the Monadnock boomed in our ears, and the signals
> from the fleet lighted the way. My husband's cousin and the
> soldier who escorted us did their best to lessen our fears.[9]

Eda and the other women stayed in the barracks, listening to the
sound of guns firing and waiting for news of their husbands from
the telegraph operator.

Tiss Palmer and some of the other wives in Marahui found it
difficult to keep up a brave front as they watched wounded being
carried from a military launch after their men had been involved
in a skirmish with the Moros. John was not among the wounded,
but it was some time before Tiss learned this. Two days later she
was again frightened when her young daughter was missing for
several hours. After much searching, the three-and-a-half-year-
old was finally located.[10]

Disease also posed a very real danger for these wives. Elizabeth
Helmick came down with dengue fever and almost died. Florence
Pinkerton recalled that her father had to arrange "to bring ice in
from Manila and put it in the bottom of the well to keep it from
melting too fast." (As the ice melted, the Filipinos accused each
other of "stealing it to take home.") Some months later Eli
Helmick had to deal with a ragging cholera epidemic which didn't
touch his family but killed many of his troops, including a married
sergeant who lived in the town.

The Helmicks' time in the Philippines was also touched by
tragedy. Florence's sister Mary had been left behind in Rhode
Island because of ill health. How difficult it must have been on
Elizabeth to have to wait months for a letter reporting on the girl's
welfare. As Elizabeth hosted a luncheon for the officers of a

visiting British battleship, the family learned of Mary's death. "While they were at the table, an orderly came in with a basket of mail from home. In it was a letter, months old, telling Mother that my sister had died," recalled Florence.

Of course, not all experiences were unpleasant ones, and Eli recalls that he had "a contented garrison. Card parties, small dances, trips up and down the river in the post launch helped to make us forget the unpleasant things."

HAWAII

Alaska, Cuba, and the Philippines were not the only overseas posts where wives followed. Some accompanied husbands to Panama and even to China where, as a part of the Allied occupation force after the Boxer Rebellion (1901), "the doughboys and their families watched the warlords come and go, saw the encroachments of the Japanese . . . [made] trips to Peking . . . occasional journeys to the Great Wall." There was also Hawaii which, as one historian states, was different "from both Panama and the Philippines in that its climate was even and salubrious . . . was a pleasant place to live in—with much the atmosphere of a summer resort."[11]

However, Bessie S. Edwards, who was with her army veterinarian husband at Schofield Barracks in 1909-1910 did not fully agree with this assessment of Hawaii as paradise.[12] She recalled a Hawaii of earlier times, and battles with red dust and red ants, and the stench of kerosene:

the large red ants were so bad, our tables, beds, etc. had to be set in tins of coal oil, and our floors of wide boards, had to be mopped up with it each day. . . . We also slept under heavy misquito [sic] nets . . . as misquitos were thick and large. Between those heavy nets, the long horned cattle trying to reach the grass under our floors, the poor sentry chasing them, and our odor of kerosene, I often wonder how we had any sleep. . . . Our houses were of boards, wide strips of screening, some tent drops, two small windows in front, one in the bedrooms, built rather high off the ground and rough inside. . . . We decided to make our front room more liveable so we papered it with flour paste and a cloth, like burlap, we bought in Honolulu. It no more than dried, when we and our guests . . . were entertained by a cracking noise we could not understand until we discovered it was beetles eating the paste.

Mrs. Edwards went on to discuss the sanitation at Schofield, indicating, "Our toilets . . . rough boards, with the wide screening all around . . . and we had to put a shovel of dirt in as we used them." However, that was not the chief problem, as she explained:

Our problem was when to use them as the prisoners came at different hours to change the cans. So it was nothing unusual to jump and yell. I do not mean to be vulgar in telling you this. It was one topic of conversation and a funny side of life here.

One luxury for many families (particularly officers' families) was the abundance of cheap and plentiful domestic help. Amahs tended the children, houseboys performed the duties of valet and butler, and laundresses were constantly busy washing and ironing.[13] Still Bessie Edwards mentions that the laundering of long white skirts or trousers, which were apparently popular items in Hawaii in the early 1900s, was a problem as the red dirt of the area left the clothes "with a reddish pink border, that even by hand washing," could not be removed. Thus, with all the availability of domestic help, maintaining a household on a "romantic island in the Pacific" was far from idyllic. Wives quickly learned that while they could share with their husbands the adventure of overseas postings, they also had to share the inconveniences.

It was said in an early history of Schofield Barracks that "if officers and their wives found life at Castner Village a trial, it was not much better for the enlisted men. Few of them had families with them and those that did had to leave them in Honolulu" (nearly a day's travel away by horseback or wagon).[14] However, there were exceptions to the rule. Carita Rodby recalled living on base as the daughter of a first sergeant.[15] Her family, along with other army families, came to Hawaii from Fort Sill, Oklahoma, in 1911.

My dad was entitled to quarters so we had a little tiny house. Five children. I don't know where Mother put them all! Later they added a bedroom. Those that were not entitled to quarters could build their own, so there were several houses that the soldiers had built themselves. They would come over [to Hawaii] and then they sent for their wives or their sweethearts, and they . . . had to go meet them with the chaplain right then—no funny business!

I know there was nothing in the houses. Our things had arrived and Dad had put a tent out in front, and all our things were stored in there. Mother was so worried about her sewing machine. We stayed with friends at Fort Ruger until Dad got the house straightened out. . . . Mother had a little two-burner kerosene stove. She had insisted on that. They told us not to bring any heavy furniture like upholstery because of termites . . . and weather. So she had this little stove, and in those days they had ammo boxes lined with zinc. She used that for a refrigerator, but I don't know where she got ice. . . . It was the only stove in the neighborhood for several weeks so whoever borrowed it in the evening invited us to dinner!

The primitive living conditions did not curtail entertaining among the officers' families. There were occasional dinners at the Moana Hotel in Honolulu and polo matches to watch. One visitor mentioned that wives, daughters and sisters were permitted to follow the men on the mandatory 100-mile physical endurance ride around the island (Oahu). When all had arrived at the night's campsite, food and music were provided, with possibly a late evening swim in the ocean.[16]

Officers' families also visited each other on base for cards and dinners, making life as pleasant as possible. "One beautiful picture will always remain with me," Bessie Edwards stated:

> as I rode [horseback] through the sweet scented pineapple fields I would ride through one shower after another but always ahead was a shower crowned by a beautiful rainbow. And on a Sunday afternoon, the Japanese maids, in their beautiful costumes, their hair bedecked in jeweled combs, some carrying fans or gay parasols would take a stroll. It was a picture of rare beauty and made one feel in a far away strange land.

And they were in faraway strange lands, these early female overseas pioneers. They coped with whatever circumstances they encountered. Perhaps Elizabeth Helmick put it best: "We must make the best out of what we have, and not pine for what we can't have," she wrote philosophically. Making the best of it was a theme that ran through most of the reminiscences of those early days overseas and would continue to be the theme of thousands of future military wives.

CHAPTER SIX

WAR AND PEACE: 1917–1941

Marie Pope Lee was frightened because telegrams meant bad news.[1] Her worst fears were realized when she read the terse message: "Husband gravely ill." Although Marie had never traveled by herself, she wired Fort Riley, Kansas, for permission to join her husband. Receiving a positive reply, she quickly boarded the train at Pueblo, Colorado, and headed east. Upon reaching her destination, she scanned the milling crowd of strangers and was relieved to find that a soldier from her husband's regiment had been sent to meet her. "Everyone was so kind to me," she recalled in an interview nearly seventy years later.

They took me by horsedrawn wagon to see him. He was in a hospital tent at Fort Riley gravely ill with measles and pneumonia. I stayed with him a while and then Sarah Ball, the wife of a soldier two cots from Earl, took me to Junction City to stay with her since there was no place for me at the fort.

Saturday morning I went back to the hospital and he seemed better. I had knit him a sweater, and he had it lying on the bed. I thought things would work out. But, when I went back Sunday morning, he had taken a turn for the worse. About 2 P.M. the doctor told me he wasn't going to get well, so I wired for Papa to come from Pueblo. Earl died that evening, two days before Christmas in 1917. Sarah helped me until Papa arrived. I had to go back from Junction City to Fort Riley to sign papers and pick up Earl's personal effects. The Army shipped his body home in a wooden box on the same train with Papa and me.

Thus at nineteen, Marie Pope became a widow—the fourth World War I widow, she thought, in Colorado. "For a long time I just couldn't believe he was gone," she sighed, her voice seeming to echo the past grief. "We had planned to go on a little ranch just east of town when he came back from overseas."

WORLD WAR I AND THE MARRIED SOLDIER

While Marie's husband was one of the casualties, out of five million Americans in uniform during World War I, relatively few married men were inducted into the army. Of 4,883,213 married men who registered with draft boards, 74.12% were deferred. Being married was a way to avoid the war, if a man wished to do so.[2]

With the advent of World War I training camps sprung up all over the nation as men were conscripted or volunteered for service in France. Housing consisted of hastily constructed barracks designed for trainees only. The few wives following their husbands had to find housing wherever they could in nearby towns or rural areas. Most times they found living conditions far from ideal.

It wasn't the war or living conditions, however, that delayed the marriage of Phyllis Weisburgh to Harry A. Levantine—it was her age.[3] Harry had already been drafted and was working in Detroit when he asked Mr. Weisburgh for his daughter's hand in marriage.

My father made us wait a year. By that time Harry had received his orders to Camp Custer in Michigan, which was about eight miles from Battle Creek. I had known Harry all my life so I had no qualms about following him to a strange place. We were married on June 17, 1917, honeymooned in Niagara Falls and then went out to Michigan a week early to look for a place to live. There was nothing. The base housed only the men. We had to find a place in town. It was so crowded with wives like me and families looking for any place to be near their husbands. Harry finally found a German family who took in boarders. It cost me $7.50 a week for room and board in this large old house. I remember the German housewife cooked heavy German meals.

I didn't like living with strangers, but I wouldn't go home. That first month was so hard. I didn't see Harry for thirty days until he got his first pass. To while away the time, I talked myself into a job at the local department store, selling boudoir caps for Christmas. My pay was $7.50 a week. Soldiers would come in to buy for their wives. One day I looked up and there was Harry standing at my counter! I hadn't seen him for so long.

After Christmas Phyllis was laid off. When she heard that the camp laundry was hiring wives and relatives of soldiers, she (like army wives in earlier times) got a job sorting officers' clean linen. Whatever she earned was sorely needed, for Harry earned only $30 a month as a private. His allotments included $15 to Phyllis and $5 sent home to his father. Phyllis recalled that the government added $15 to the monthly allotment check, but she didn't remember why.

In order to keep the laundry job, all employees were required to be vaccinated. By the time I went home the day I got my shots, my arm was killing me. I was so sick I couldn't get out of bed the next day. My sister came from Chicago to take care of me, and Harry sneaked out of camp whenever he could to see me. I finally got well. We were at Camp Custer nine months. Harry was in the first draft, and his group was kept to train those drafted later. His last stop in

the States was at Camp Mills, Long Island. I followed him
out there and stayed with an aunt. When an officer saw me
waiting at the base gate, he came over and said, "You can't
see your husband. They can't leave the base." I waited;
Harry walked across the field, and I sent him back loaded
down with food from all the relatives.

Harry survived the war because his captain "mostly had him
drawing maps." While not an artist as a young man, Harry's life
came full circle. After his retirement, he began painting vibrant
desert landscapes. At the time of her interview, his widow Phyllis
was surrounded by his oil paintings in her Los Angeles apartment.

Wives who before the war had followed their men to stateside
and overseas assignments were now not allowed to accompany
the troops to France. However, Captain George Patton (later
commanding general of the U.S. Third Army during World War
II) wrote extensively to his wife, Beatrice, encouraging her to
make every attempt to join him.

(July 16, 1917) . . . the only thing to do is to put pres-
sure . . . on the secretary of state so you can come. Not as
a nurse but straight out. . . . I disapprove your coming as a
red cross nurse for there is no telling but we would be so far
apart we could never meet. . . . There is not the *least* doubt
that with proper influence you can get pasports [sic]. Use
the influence. . . . Remember you must come and you must
not come as a nurse.[4]

Patton mentioned to Beatrice that other wives were in France
(Mrs. Bertie McCormick of Chicago, Mrs. Ester Johnson of New
York, and Mrs. E. B. Krumbhaar of Philadelphia, the wife of a
Red Cross doctor). However, nothing came of the Pattons' efforts,
even though Beatrice had sent a telegram to George asking him
to enlist General Pershing's aid in obtaining a passport for her.

Darling Beat: I got your wire asking me to get General P. to give his consent. He can't do it because it was on his advice that the order [prohibiting wives from coming to France] was issued. You see the British had to send back 60,000 women who came over with the Canadians.[5]

Despite her determined efforts, Mrs. Patton and most other wives were forced to remain behind. World War I was the first of four major conflicts fought outside the United States where women would become "waiting wives." No longer was the wife needed to cook, sew, and nurse for the army in battle; her place by the side of her military husband in the twentieth century would be relegated to peacetime activities only.

OCCUPATION DUTY

After the armistice in November 1918, the army needed men for the occupation in Europe. Mary Leontine Bartow's husband was one of those drafted from college who would see service in the army of occupation in Germany.[6] "We were both at the University of Washington State when Donald was called up," she recalled. "It was the twelfth of June, 1919. I was able to follow him to San Antonio where we got married. He went with the Fifth Infantry to Germany—of course, they weren't taking the wives—so I went back to Tacoma to wait until I could go."

In 1920, Mary was finally allowed to join her husband. "We sailed on a troopship out of Hoboken, New Jersey. All staterooms required passengers to walk outside to get to the dining room, whether it was wet or dry. We were wet and uncomfortable quite often." However, when she finally reached Germany, she and her husband found living accommodations improved greatly and were "very comfortable in two rooms in a wealthy German home. I never did any of the cooking as our maid fixed food for us in the kitchen."

Although the Bartow's first son was born at the military hospital in Koblenz, that didn't stop her from traveling. She felt that her husband's captain salary was "lavish in those days," and many times she and other army wives in the area toured Europe. "It was exciting to travel over all of Europe. We took our babies and maids and went traveling. We had lots of money, both officer and enlisted, compared to the Europeans. When we returned to the States we filled a whole transport. It was a great life."

Not all officers' wives were as fortunate as Mrs. Bartow, however. When Commander William F. "Bull" Halsey was sent to Germany as a naval attaché in 1922, he had a difficult time finding affordable accommodations for his family. In those days of Germany's postwar inflation, Commander Halsey and his wife, Fan (for Fanny), finally found an apartment in suburban Berlin. "For lack of fuel there was no heat or hot water, but there were plenty of quilts and blankets. When the weather was especially cold the Halseys either stayed with friends who had heat or covered themselves with bedclothes." The family did have a housekeeper who managed to do some cooking with available electricity. A good portion of the time Fan and the children were coping with these problems alone as Commander Halsey was often away at conferences.[7]

Back in the United States, the military in the 1920s was faced with many inconsistencies. Because a large portion of the civilian population had been touched by the war and were aware that a soldier's life was not an easy one, most civilians, at least for a while, were sympathetic to the military man. While some officers overseas may have been living comfortably on their salaries, military pay had not kept up with war prices in the United States, and both officers and soldiers were finding expenses outrunning income. However, in May 1920, Congress granted a twenty percent temporary pay raise to enlisted men and additional yearly pay for officers depending on rank. Colonels and lieutenant colonels, for example received $600 per year extra, majors drew $840, while second lieutenants received only $420.[8]

In June 1920, the National Defense Act called for a standing army of up to 280,000 officers and men, with improved training for all ranks. When the temporary pay relief expired in 1922, it was decided to establish a more modern pay scale for the army. Officers would receive a base pay, a rations allowance and a rental allowance. Some saw this as inequitable, for an officer with a family received more than an officer who was single. (Allowances ranged from a low of $20 to a high of $120 a month, according to a man's marital status and his length of time in the service.) Although there were no allowances for enlisted men as they were expected (and generally required) to remain single, the monthly wage was increased for the upper grades. Travel pay for officers' families was even established.[9] These financial improvements must certainly have made the choice of a military career more appealing.

The euphoria did not last, however. Public attitudes were changing and questions were being asked about the need for so many men in uniform. Peace and prosperity were on the horizon and thoughts of war were far behind. In addition, the media and various organizations reminded people of the horrors of modern war. The public's attitude was that the United States should never become involved in another war, and the American abhorrence of a large standing army diluted Congressional support for the military.

As a result, shortly after the new pay scale had been passed (over the objections of the Secretary of War), Congress reduced the army to 175,000 officers and men. This meant an immediate reduction in force of 600 line officers and more than 100,000 enlisted personnel. In addition, all promotions were frozen until January 1, 1923.[10] Such reduction in forces would occur after national crises and conflict for the remainder of the twentieth century.

By the middle of 1924, the scarcity of officers forced officers to change stations so often to meet the needs of the various units that travel costs ate up a good portion of the military budget. Due to budget limitations, improvements in living conditions for the men themselves and their families became negligible.[11] As the world settled into a time of relative peace followed by the Great

Depression, the United States military entered a period of stag-
nation which remained unchanged until World War II.

THE ENLISTED IN A PEACETIME ARMY

During the 1920s, a gradual change took place in the attitude
of the military toward dependents. Families were still not given
much consideration, since most junior officers and virtually all
enlisted men were expected to and did stay single. Yet in 1925,
government policy was revised, permitting enlisted men to marry,
although up until World II an enlisted man ranked E-4 or less still
"could be discharged for the convenience of the government if
he married without the written permission of his superior officer."[12] (Well into the 1960s, enlisted men were still expected to
request permission to marry.) However, the fact that enlisted men
could officially marry led to a growing number of enlisted
dependents.

As more and more dependents descended on the bases, they
often had to endure substandard lifestyles. In December 1925, the
Infantry Journal published a major exposé on military housing
by its Washington correspondent, E. B. Johns. Johns told of
NCOs and their families "occupying abandoned black laborers'
shacks at Fort Benning [Georgia] and of officers resigning rather
than accepting the uninhabitable quarters offered them."[13] Various accounts indicate that both officers' and enlisteds' housing
many times consisted of unpainted, dingy, overcrowded, sometimes damp rooms, shared bathhouses and toilets and inadequate
sanitation.

Those married enlisted men who were below the rank of NCO
"constituted a class of soldier that always lived on the edge of
poverty." Still, enlisted received permission to and did marry.
When Raymond G. Alvord (who retired as a first sergeant in 1955)
got married in the 1930s, he "had no trouble getting permission;
the catch was you had to live within your means. If the company
commander got one letter from a collection agency, that was it;
you couldn't reenlist." Alvord supplemented his income of $50

a month with an off-duty job and considered himself fortunate to be living in government quarters consisting of living room, bedroom, shared bath, and community kitchen "three floors down."[14]

In March 1931, Brigadier General William P. Jackson, in a report on married enlisted men, complained:

> They exist in squalid surroundings, in dingy dark, over-crowded rooms where the simplest rules of sanitation and hygiene are difficult if not impossible of accomplishment. Their health, morale, vitality and efficiency is bound to suffer.[15]

This wretched condition of married enlisted was not merely a direct result of the economic depression of the 1930s. It was also the result of "low pay, poor housing, ignorance, and lack of official concern."[16]

An extensive staff study followed Jackson's report, but no one suggested the army take action to correct the problem. While the study recognized that the situation had reached the point where enlisted men might not be effective in army field service, it indicated that the army would have to be cautious in seeking a solution to the problem because "present economic situation makes this an inopportune time for the War Department to take action which might be construed as forcing married men out of the service."[17]

Of course, some commanders did help the married enlisted and his family with housing. For example, Major General Johnson Hagood of the Seventh Corps turned over "abandoned wartime structures, one story affairs that had been used as barracks, hospital wards, warehouses, etc." to the married enlisted. The enlisted men then repaired and redecorated these makeshift quarters.[18]

Good nutrition was also a major problem for enlisted families. General Jackson's study showed that undernourishment was ". . . frequently observed, resulting in at least one instance at this station [Madison Barracks, Sackett Harbor, New York] in hospitalization due to weakness." Jackson noted that some enlisted families became objects of charity, citing an incident when officers of the fort donated nineteen dollars "to provide fuel and milk for a new mother and her baby."[19] Many times the row of enlisted married quarters on base was known as "Hungry Hill."[20]

As late as 1937, with one-fifth of the enlisted men in the army married, only one-quarter of these married men were authorized quarters. The remaining men (approximately 18,000) did not receive quarters, quarters allowance, or subsistence allowance, which was authorized for enlisted men in the top three grades. As a result, an estimated 45,000 unwanted (and according to the army's view, unneeded) dependents experienced "want and suffering . . . due to lack of proper clothing, housing, food and sanitary conditions." The army concluded that it was allowing "too much discretion to the local commander with regard to permitting the reenlistment of married enlisted men under grade three who had married without permission or had families they could not support properly on their Army pay."[21] On June 7, 1939, the army Chief of Staff toughened regulations as follows:

Enlisted men except in grades 1, 2, or 3, who marry without the written permission of the Corps Area or Department Commander after June 30, 1939, will be discharged without delay for the convenience of the Government and will not be reenlisted.[22]

While this order stopped the growth of lower enlisted families, it did nothing to help the young enlisted soldier who was already married and living on "Hungry Hill." He and his family would struggle on until war came once again and the American public softened its attitude toward the needs of the military.

THE CHANGING "ARISTOCRACY"

Until World War I, most officers were graduates of West Point or Annapolis. Many carried on a family tradition of several generations of men in arms, and many had personal incomes aside from their military pay. However, additional officers had been needed for the campaign in Europe, and conscription made officers of men from all walks of life. After demobilization, some of these men remained in this new career. Since most of these men had only their monthly pay, maintaining the "style of an officer" could be difficult.

For the officer's wife of the 1920s and 1930s, life was lived with as much grace as her husband's rank and income permitted. Protocol was critically important; distinction between the ranks became sharper. It was a time of calling cards and engraved invitations to afternoon teas, gala balls, and elaborate receptions. The social side of military life took on an even greater importance than it had in the past, creating for the wives diversion from boredom and anxiety over their individual social successes or failures. The success of an officer's career was closely linked to his wife's ability to entertain.

Also, the size and location of quarters could have an impact on how an officer was viewed by the military community. Sometimes he might be able to minipulate the "old boy" network and control where he lived, but more often his residence and location was based upon his rank and seniority. On some of the older bases, where officer housing had been in existence for years, upgrading and remodeling was accomplished. While not palaces, many of these homes were more than adequate. Some officers' quarters had a spare room off the kitchen (and later a bath) for the family maid. Probably the most posh living for military officers of the time was overseas:

For the army wife and her husband, too, as well as for the bachelor, servants were plentiful and cheap. Houseboys took care of the officers from changing buttons to ironing the stiffly starched uniforms always laid out. . . . The *amah* rode herd on the children. The cook could do amazing things with canned milk.[23]

If an officer couldn't obtain quarters on-base for his family, he at least had an allowance to help defray the cost of off-post housing. Of course, this quarters allowance for officers by no means guaranteed stylish living, whether on- or off-base. What type of quarters an officer had depended on his rank, where he was stationed, and the availability of housing. For some home was expensive, uncomfortable, and dreary; for others it was the epitome of gracious living.

When, in 1923, First Lieutenant James "Jimmy" Doolittle was assigned to a group of six army men attending the Massachusetts Institute of Technology (MIT) in Cambridge, he soon found that his budget was severely stretched by the cost of housing his wife Joe and their two small children. Joe Doolittle finally found a complete floor in a three-family house, although it was on the other side of Boston from MIT. Rent was $65 a month, which "subtracted considerably from her husband's $160 a month Army check."[24]

At West Point in 1920, General Omar Bradley noted in his autobiography that, as a junior officer, he and his wife Mary felt lucky to get into former bachelor officers' apartments "crudely converted to accommodate married officers, some with children." Bradley also mentioned renting a small frame house near Fort Benning, Georgia, in 1924. Assured by the landlord that Georgia winters were mild, he and Mary failed to note that there was no central heating. Remarked the General, "Night after night I huddled in the frigid kitchen reviewing my studies in extremely uncomfortable circumstances, silently cursing the landlord."[25]

For the George C. Marshalls, a 1924 assignment to China was an enjoyable hiatus. Lily Marshall

had ten servants to look after their quarters—she was able to devote her time to being a senior officer's wife, keeping the other wives occupied and happy, overseeing the welfare of the men. Her spare time was filled with trips to Peking or the seaside and shopping expeditions in the bazaars. She was almost sorry when Marshall's tour of duty came to an end, describing it in letters to relatives at home as one great big "three-years shopping trip."[26]

In a 1989 interview, eighty-eight-year-old Eva Moore Higgins also recalled the excitement, luxury, and relaxation, as well as some of the problems, connected with overseas army travel in the 1920s.[27] When her captain husband received orders to Hawaii, she assumed the family would be traveling together. However, Captain Higgins was assigned to arrange transport for army troops also traveling to Hawaii and was only able to drop off his wife and infant daughter at the military ship in New York.

We were the only females on the ship for two days. Finally some other wives arrived, as well as the men and we were able to set sail.

I remember there was a terrible storm shortly after we left port. I didn't lose my dinner but we were all unable to do much. The stewardess came into the cabin and asked if she could help me. I said, "If you'll just put the baby over there in the middle of that bunk, that will be a big help." Soon the storm was over, and then we all relaxed and had a fine time.

There were just two of us on board with babies. Of course, there was no water in our staterooms, so the stewards would bring in buckets of water for us to wash diapers. Then we would just hang the diapers along the ship's railings to dry. I imagine it looked pretty funny, this ocean liner sailing across the blue with diapers flapping in the sea breeze.

We sailed down the East Coast and through the Panama Canal to San Francisco. Then it took us nearly twenty days to go from San Francisco to Honolulu, but when we arrived we were so pleased to be met by friends we had known before. Of course, in those days, they all brought leis of

gorgeous flowers to us. We were quartered at Fort Shafter.
It was a lovely place.

Not all officers' families were as fortunate as Mrs. Higgins.
At Camp Lewis, Washington, one officer and his family opted to
accept quarters in a former dental clinic. The first floor consisted
of two rooms at opposite ends of what had been a waiting room.
As there was no equipment in the kitchen, all cooking had to be
done on two small portable electric grills. The one good point to
these quarters—the reason the family had selected them—was that
they were in one of the few buildings in the brigade area which
had indoor plumbing.[28]

Perhaps Bull Halsey's quarters were the most unusual. When
Captain Halsey was ordered to the Naval Academy at Annapolis
in 1927, as commanding officer of the *USS Reina Mercedes*, he
found that his residence was a former cruiser captured during the
Spanish–American War. "This will never do," his wife Fan said
when she saw the old hulk where she and her family were
expected to live. "I will never live here. It isn't a fit place for
human beings." (How many military wives through the years
have said that?) Like most military wives, Fan relented, and with
the help of the cook, steward, and stewardsman scoured and
decorated the quarters until they were livable.[29]

For each wife, military life held both similar and different
experiences. Harriet ("Muffy") Olson detailed the grandeur of
the early years overseas, living a life of luxury as well as
experiencing the dangers of war. As she explained it, her life
story could almost be told in twenty-year segments—twenty years
as an "army brat," twenty years as an army wife, and her last
two decades as a "retired" military wife and successful realtor
with her own business.[30]

As an army brat, she first went to the Philippines in 1919, where
her family lived in a big set of quarters in Manila. The family
had a Chinese *amah*, houseboy, cook, and *lavandera* (laundry
woman), and was typical of many officers' families living overseas during that era.

My greatest memory there was long walks in Luneta Park with my brother and our Chinese *amah*. However, my father's favorite story happened one day when, returning from work, he approached our home and watched an old Filipino driving a pony-drawn cart full of junk with two children sitting on the back. Their legs were hanging off the back and they were trying to see how far they could spit. He suddenly realized the one child was a Filipino, but the other was his own daughter—me.

We soon moved to Corregidor where my father was Quartermaster of the Harbor Defenses of Manilla and Subic bays. Life on Corregidor in those days was a paradise for kids. We lived there for three years. I was eight years old when we left so those years were a vivid memory for me. My brother was eighteen months older than I, and we had free reign over Topside, Middleside, and some exposure to Bottomside. Topside was mainly for ranking officers, and since my dad was a major, that's where we lived. (In those days . . . a major was quite a rank!) We lived in a huge concrete building and had the top floor. It had exterior cement stairs with a wide porch that ran all the way around.

The trolley ran from Topside to Middleside to Bottomside, and my brother and I spent a great deal of time riding the trolley up and down. Middleside was where the junior grade officers and non-coms lived, and lots of our friends were there.

In 1939, Harriet's father (Major General Richard J. Marshall, who would become MacArthur's deputy chief of staff when the Philippines were invaded and who escaped to Australia) received orders to the Philippines again, at the request of General MacArthur. As her father was in charge of the Water Transportation Branch, which included the Army Transport Service, he arranged for his family to sail aboard the ship *Fort Leonard Wood* from New York to join him. Because it was a commercial ship it was luxurious, and the Marshalls had large staterooms with full baths. It took them three weeks of sailing through the Panama Canal to reach Honolulu. There the family transferred to the old *U.S.A.F. Grant*, a sturdy ship without the glamor of the previous one and with shared bathroom facilities:

Anyone who traveled on the *Grant* in those days will well remember George, the black man, who delivered your one bucket of fresh water to rinse off with after bathing in saltwater.

Life on the *Grant* may not have been luxurious, but it was more fun than any luxury trip you could buy. A daily bulletin let everyone know the activities of the day. . . . I was about to turn sixteen so I was most interested in the social life. . . . The daily bulletin also gave news. We were all concerned about Japanese subs in the fall of 1939 and just where the war would start next.

Manila, in 1939, was exciting and beautiful. The economy meant everyone still had a house full of servants. Most higher-ranking officers also had drivers, not just for convenience but Americans caught in traffic violations were in real trouble. Parties were lavish . . . schools and offices were out at noon (they started very early in the morning because of the heat), so the afternoons were full of golf, tennis or swimming. The Army-Navy Club was the most popular meeting place.

Boat days—called *bienvedidas*—were for meeting the incoming service families. As the transport arrived and flower leis were slipped on the newcomers, everyone then moved to the Army-Navy Club and started a day of partying to welcome the new families and to get to know those in your age groups. It also meant the latest news from the States!

As the end of 1940 arrived, more navy wives were being sent home to the States, and the concern for war began in earnest. Next were the army wives, and then it was no longer the same carefree place.

Nor would it be the same carefree place for many years to come. As the peacetime military abruptly adopted a wartime footing, the genteel life of the officer's wife altered also. And, back in the United States, a generation of civilian women who had never given a second thought to the military would soon take up the practice of campfollowing as they attempted to stay with their draftee husbands until overseas orders arrived.

CHAPTER SEVEN

WOMEN AND WAR:
1941–1972

A light snow softened the Christmas Eve afternoon as Lucille Giordano Ritzus stepped off the train in Lafayette, Indiana, eager to spend a few months with her husband Steve before he would be sent overseas.[1] It was December 1941, and for Lucille, as for millions of American women, life as a military wife had been forced upon her. In the years of peace between the two world wars, most American women had husbands they sent off every day to ordinary jobs. For most couples the military lifestyle was not part of their plans. "I had never thought about the armed forces one way or another," Lucille commented. "Most of the girls I grew up with had never imagined being married to an army man."

Suddenly we were all caught up in a war. My husband was drafted into the navy and sent to Purdue University at Lafayette for training as an electrician. We hadn't been married too long, so I wanted to be with him for as long as possible. As I walked around the city that Christmas Eve afternoon, waiting to meet Steve after his classes, I felt very lost and alone. As I passed a beauty shop, I decided to go in and ask for a job. The owners hired me immediately.

Steve had rented a hotel room for us for three days, but he had to return to the barracks after the holidays. We couldn't find a place for me to rent. There was simply nothing available! I had my job and didn't want to return home—didn't want to leave him since none of us knew what would happen in the coming days. Finally, I met a woman who ran a small hotel down the street from the one we had stayed in. She didn't have any vacant rooms, but she told me I could sleep on a cot in the hotel's kitchen and share her bathroom. That was my "room" for the three months Steve was in training. Still I tried not to mind. I was young and didn't think much about the way I was living. And it was so good to be able to see him occasionally.

Lucille Ritzus was like so many others caught up in the drastic changes brought about by the world conflict. Almost everyone had either a family member or a neighbor involved in the fighting. This meant that the numbers involved in the war effort were far more than just the 8,300,000 in the armed forces at peak strength in 1945.[2] Those left behind participated by conserving: sometimes enforced by the hated rationing coupons, sometimes by making do with substitutes, such as "butter" which had to be colored with a yellow capsule to make it look more palatable.

With the men being rapidly sent to overseas assignments, wives were again left anxiously waiting at home. Many women took over defense jobs and were never again quite as happy only being homemakers. Many say the sweeping changes in the American family, changes which would have an impact on the military family system in future decades, began in those tumultuous war years. Although most wives were not close to dangerous zones, all felt the effects of the conflict.

IN HARM'S WAY

Because of anticipated hostilities with Japan, most military dependents were sent home to the United States from overseas bases in the Pacific. However, not all made it out of the danger area. In July 1942, Kay Walter, the bride of Marine Sergeant Henry "Buddy" Walter, was reported to have been captured in

Manila by the Japanese and placed in a Philippine internment camp. Her husband was listed as missing after fighting on Corregidor.[3] There is no record of whether or not she survived the imprisonment.

A number of wives were also with their husbands in Hawaii during the bombing of Pearl Harbor. Leontine Thodarson Briggs witnessed the attack from Pacific Heights, high above Pearl Harbor.[4] Her husband, Mark, had been in the reserves since their marriage in 1935. Once the bombs fell, he reverted to active status as a second lieutenant. Mrs. Briggs's memories remain vivid:

> We were at the home of Dr. and Mrs. Gregory when we saw the planes circling the harbor and heard the bombs. From the heights we could see the debris fly up as Hickam was bombed. Turning on the radio we heard the voice of Waverly Edwards of *Hawaii Calls* saying, "This is war. This is the real thing. Take cover." My husband Mark said, "I have to report." In a moment he was gone.

Because she had lived in Hawaii since 1931, following her graduation from Oregon State University, and taught physical education at the Honolulu YWCA, Mrs. Briggs knew enough of the local people not to be fully caught up in the hysteria that followed the bombing.

> High feelings ran against the Japanese. In those days you didn't have a live-in maid but a cleaning woman. Rumors flew that the maids would kill every lady on the block. But having worked at the YW, I knew the Japanese. . . . Yet the rumors persisted. One was that we were supposedly overrun by eight transports so I was told to take water, my pistol, and climb the hills of Tantalus [above Honolulu] to save myself in order that I wouldn't be killed.

With the bombing, life changed drastically. Blackouts and curfews were imposed. Mrs. Briggs recalled painting lightbulbs black and then scraping a thin sliver of paint off each bulb to provide some illumination. She and her husband brought water, food, and mattresses into the garage and made a fortress out of it. Extra mattresses were placed on the garage roof to give some protection from the bombs which were expected to fall on the civilian population. Other mattresses were piled on the dining room floor, and about twenty people "camped out" in their home for three nights following the bombing.

> Food was not important because we couldn't get it. We did without. Values and ideas change a lot when you are under pressure. The value of money changes greatly. If you have money, you can get food, of course—but money doesn't buy safety. Personally, I can't ever remember being really afraid for I never thought I'd be killed. We seemed so isolated in Honolulu. But the war changed so much in the islands.

Since civilian patients in Queen's Hospital were being evacuated to make room for the wounded, Mrs. Briggs was asked to take in a female doctor who was recovering from a heart attack. The army commandeered Punahou, a private school, and for a year classes were held in private homes and churches. Sand Island was turned into a big concentration camp, holding hundreds of Japanese and German internees.

While Phyllis Thompson Wright, wife of naval officer Jerry Wright (who eventually became an admiral), was not in a danger zone herself, she was helping out as a volunteer with the Navy Relief in San Francisco, where evacuees from Honolulu were sent. When alerted, representatives of the Red Cross, the American Women's Voluntary Services (AWVS), and Navy Relief, as well as medical personnel and ambulances, met each ship evacuating military wives and children from Honolulu. Mrs. Wright described the destitute condition of some of the incoming navy and marine families:

The sadness of some cases is still clear in my mind. Many were the poor young women whose husbands had been killed on December 7 who were returning with their children. They were dazed with sorrow and wan from the fear and discomfort of that slow voyage across submarine-infested waters. With each cabin crammed to overflowing, far beyond its normal capacity, fresh water had to be restricted; and each passenger was permitted only two buckets of water a day with which to wash everything.[5]

Because of lack of water, impetigo raged aboard each ship. After living in the tropics, most children lacked winter clothing. The various agencies collected warm clothes for both the wives and children and sent some warm clothing back to Honolulu for the next scheduled evacuation ship.

Tropical clothing was not needed by Elva J. Maughan, who spent the war years in the much harsher climes of Alaska.[6]

My husband Chuck and I left the United States in June of 1941, headed for Kodiak, Alaska, where he would work with Morrison-Knudson to help build Fort Greeley. I was pregnant, and my parents were fearful that their grandchild would be born on someone's kitchen table. However, on September 29, 1941, Randall (the Maughans' son) and the noon whistle took off together in a very modern little hospital. . . .

Came Pearl Harbor! We discovered Randy's first tooth and went shopping for blackout curtains. Chuck was drafted shortly after Christmas and did his basic training there at Fort Greeley. Not long after that the military wives were evacuated. Since I had not come there as a military wife, I was allowed to stay. With a good baby sitter next door, I was asked to come out and help run the Quartermaster office. I did this until June of 1945—VE Day.

CAMPFOLLOWING AT HOME

With the massive military expansion needed to fight the war, a large number of married men with dependents were inducted. Recognizing the economic problems of these families, in 1942 Congress passed the Servicemen's Dependents Allowance Act, which augmented the pay of enlisted men with dependents by providing an additional "$28 monthly for a wife, $40 for a wife and child, $10 for each additional child." *Yank* magazine brought the good news to the wives:

> Whether she's working or not, the soldier's wife comes in for a $50 monthly allotment under the recent pay bill. . . . The government takes $22 [if you sign the application] out of your pay, couples it with $28 from its own pocket and mails it to mama. [If no requisition filled out] . . . the little woman is out in the cold.[7]

The office of Dependency Benefits, located in Newark, New Jersey, kept control records on all family allowances (support for dependents of enlisted men going overseas) and family allotments, which was pay voluntarily assigned by both officers and enlisted men to their dependents. Under this program, the government contributed approximately two dollars for every one contributed by a soldier, up to a maximum of $60 per month.[8] The initiation of these allotments was a vital morale factor to the wives left at home or those wives and families temporarily accompanying the men to camps throughout the States.

With this financial help, many wives and children elected to follow their husbands from camp to camp in the United States. It was a trying pilgrimage: Gasoline was rationed, worn out tires were almost impossible to replace, trains were jammed, housing was scarce to nonexistent. A hall bedroom with kitchen privileges could be a luxury, and some families had to do with semiconverted garages or henhouses.[9]

One present-day army wife recalled that she and her mother alternately lived with grandparents and followed her father:

> We lived all over the States in some really weird places, where bases no longer exist. Father was in the Army Air Corps. . . . I remember a handmade caravan-type home. Mom told me of places they lived that were on the lists and recommended [by the military as satisfactory housing] . . . one place had a crack in the commode and they had to move.

Although wives were of all ages, Mary Owens, age 22, typified many of the young World War II wives. She followed her husband to the Aberdeen Proving Grounds in Maryland and joined many other wives of soldiers deployed to this training center. Some of the wives were lucky enough to get jobs testing and inspecting guns and equipment, earning $25–$30 a week, which at that time was considered "good dough."[10]

It was immediately after Christmas Eve mass in December, 1941, at Camp Barkley, Texas, that Nadine Ruspini and Harley Morton were married.[11] Morton had gone into the army the previous January when the draft was begun. Nadine had been teaching in Colorado and was warned by her principal that "if you get married, it makes your teaching contract null and void." However, Nadine was not deterred, and left by bus as soon as Christmas vacation began.

> I guess I never considered how my parents felt, either. Here I was the oldest and first to be getting married, and they would not be at the ceremony. We were lucky, though, as Harley's cousin Max was also at Camp Barkley. So we did have some family at the ceremony. I was the only woman present in that whole base chapel that Christmas eve, among a large crowd of men. There was an organist and the chapel was all decorated with greens; it smelled so Christmasy and was so pretty. The organist and quite a few of the men

attending mass stayed on for our vows, which made it appear more like an ordinary ceremony. I didn't have a wedding gown. In fact, I was planning on wearing something that I already had in my closet, but my mother insisted that for my wedding I should have a new outfit. We went shopping the night before I left Colorado. So I wore a little blue crepe dress and a matching hat but didn't carry a bouquet. At the time it didn't seem strange. After all, it was wartime.

The reason they got married then was that Harley's division, the Thunderbird Division, was scheduled to go overseas. After the brief Christmas honeymoon, Nadine returned alone to Colorado. Shortly thereafter, Morton was accepted for Officer Candidate School and did not receive an overseas assignment until much later. When he was commissioned a second lieutenant in October 1942, Nadine joined him at Fort Polk near Little Rock, Arkansas, where they were able to get a room in a lawyer's home. "I don't think there were any quarters on the base," recalled Nadine. "These were tent camps; there were no quarters because this was wartime. Most wives had to find a place to live in nearby towns."

Several months later, Lieutenant Morton was reassigned to Fort Robinson, Louisiana, and Nadine remembered that they went there by military convoy:

One of the officers needed to take his car, and so I drove it. The young soldier boys kept getting lost, so for a goodly while in the dark of the night, I led that convoy . . . through the swamps. . . . Harley was in a jeep racing up and down, making sure everyone stayed together. . . . As far as I know there were no enlisted wives in the convoy, but there was another officer's wife named Lee. We remained friends for a very long time afterwards.

To begin with, the Mortons lived in Alexandria, Louisiana, in a bedroom with kitchen privileges. Later they and another army couple rented a house in LeCount. By then it was Christmas of 1943, so the military "gypsies" packed up their pots and pans, their bedding, and their Christmas tree, and took a taxi to their new home.

For many World War II wives, campfollowing would consist mainly of short, hurried visits from "home" to the stateside camps where their husbands were moved—brief reunions in a chaotic world. Typical of these wives was Myrthel Strand Fuller.[12] Her husband Bill had taken Myrthel and their small son from Maryland back to their original home in Evanston, Illinois. Then Bill began his tour in the army. As with many young wives of that period, Myrthel gave birth to the couple's daughter while her husband was away.

When Barb was a little over three months old, I was able to leave her and my son with my sister for a few days and join Bill at Fort Benning, Georgia. I specifically remember one incident because it made me so angry. When I arrived at the train depot in Georgia, Bill met me, and we started to get a taxi to take us to the hotel where a room was reserved. But, because Bill was an enlisted man, and there was an officer who would also be riding in the cab, Bill was not allowed to ride with us. The officer and I rode to the hotel in complete silence. Bill had to take a bus.

In the winter of 1944, Myrthel left Evanston to spend some time with Bill in New York City. When she arrived at the hotel where her husband had made a reservation for the couple, she was shown to a "tiny room with only a small cot." Immediately Myrthel went back to the reservation desk and told the clerk that the accommodations were not acceptable because her husband would be arriving shortly. The hotel management "were very nice and gave us the loveliest accommodations."

Bill soon came and we had a wonderful evening—took in a play, went to dinner and then danced to the music of Vincent

Lopez, who had a well-known band at that time. When Bill left to return to camp that night, he told me he would see me the next night. But I never saw him again, until after the war.

Myrthel waited at the hotel for four or five days, hoping for word from her husband. Later she learned that his company had been alerted for overseas duty, and all outside communication had been banned. She and several wives heard rumors that their men would be "shipping out" on the Queen Mary. Realizing that the ship would pass by the Statue of Liberty, Myrthel and the other wives took the ferry out to the Statue.

There we stood, crying and waving as the huge ship passed. It was a very, very sad time for me. I remember the tears and how brokenhearted we all were. Only later did I learn that all my crying and waving was to no avail. Bill was not on the Queen Mary! Now we can look back at this incident and laugh. But then, it was very sad, and what could I do? I returned to Evanston and waited for his letters, most of which were so badly censored that they didn't make any sense at all. Still, they told me he was alive.

Placida (Flossie) Lucero Sorrell married her husband on December 8, 1944 (shortly after he returned to the United States from a wartime tour in England), and the couple left immediately for a new assignment in Laredo, Texas.[13] The Sorrells lived in one room in a private home, without kitchen privileges. "I went to work in a restaurant," Flossie stated, "so we could afford to eat." After four months, they were sent to Gowan Army Air Base at Boise, Idaho. "We were on the train from the southern tip of Texas, in a chair car, clear to Boise. I can't even remember how many days it was, but it seemed forever." After nine months, the couple were again on the move—to Denver, Colorado. The nomadic life had begun and would continue throughout the Sorrells' military career.

While most World War II wives did their campfollowing in the United States, some wives eventually went overseas. Clarice Matthewson Corboy recalled her trip by train from Valparaiso, Indiana, to San Francisco to catch a convoy for Honolulu.[14] She considered herself lucky to be able to join her husband while the war was in progress. It was May 1945, when she boarded the ship with three children—four- and six-year-old sons and a nine-month-old daughter.

> There were seven in our tiny cabin, with no bedsheets, and an older woman who was not much used to young children. We had been allowed to bring on board the *Permanente* (a cement ship) only what we could carry. There were two or three seatings for meals and only two bathrooms on each deck, if I recall correctly. Of course, with the baby, diapers presented a problem although we did have some kind of disposable ones at that time. Still we all tried to maintain good spirits even though we were confined to the ship for a week in the harbor at San Francisco before setting sail.

Needless to say, Mrs. Corboy was very happy to be met at dockside in Hawaii by her husband, a navy doctor.

Lucille Ritzus again traveled to be with her husband when he was returned in late 1944 to a hospital near San Francisco. She stayed in a hotel for several weeks and then was "fortunate to get a room in a private home in Oakland which allowed me to visit Steve each day in San Leandro." Lucille recalled the celebration at the end of the war. "Everyone was simply wild. People were shouting and dancing in the streets. Cable cars were overturned. There was a great deal of joy."

DURING THE OCCUPATION

With the end of the war in August 1945, families followed the soldiers overseas into Allied or occupied countries. For some it was luxurious living in commandeered mansions. Others rented whatever they could find and adjusted to French plumbing, German language, electric adapters needed for American appliances, "the reek of Korean and Japanese rice paddies fertilized with human feces, or Okinawan 'stealee boys' who could swipe the buttons off your shirt while you talked with them."[15] Shortly after World War II, dependents' allowances were taken away as Congress attempted to revert to a single man's military. A husband's rank and military salary greatly affected a family's lifestyle.

Bernadine V. Lee left Colorado with her three children in September 1946, to join her captain husband. There were 840 wives waiting at Fort Lawton near Seattle for the Matson luxury liner *Monterey*. Rumors were rife that in Japan there would be no meat, butter, eggs, or orange juice, and that "The Japs are likely to take potshots at us from dark buildings. . . ."[16] However, things were not as rumored and Mrs. Lee was particularly surprised when she saw her new home which was

a western-style, two-story frame house with a garden wall—a house with gracious old trees, a yard friendly in shrubs and flowers . . . four servants . . . with many smiles and bows . . . electric stove and electric refrigerator, toaster, waffle iron, coffee percolator, dishes, silverware, table linen, and even curtains . . . two bathrooms, one with a tile bathtub; four bedrooms.[17]

Mrs. Lee added that while their home was not the most modest in Tokyo, neither was it the most lavish. Some of their friends lived in eighteen-room villas requisitioned from wealthy Japanese; others lived in Quonset huts or small apartments. The Lees were able to get their accommodations based on seniority, rank, and the number of family members. Her husband's twenty-five years in the Army, plus the three children, were a big help. While not everything was rosy in Japan immediately after the war, Mrs. Lee encouraged other wives to "hesitate no longer" in following their husbands to occupation duty.[18]

General William C. Chase wrote that he and his wife were quartered in a big modern house in the western suburbs of Kinchijoji near the Konganei Golf Course in Tokyo. The house had belonged to a Japanese businessman who had moved to the beach during the American fire raids over Tokyo. It was a "modernistic structure . . . with glass on one whole side . . . several patio gardens, and to top it all, a roof garden from which one could see Mt. Fuji."[19] Of course, most service families lived in much more modest quarters.

Jeanne D'Arcy Vaughn felt she had "such an adventure" when she left her home in Providence, Rhode Island, for the first time to be one of the first wives to sail in 1946, from Fort Lawton, Washington, to join her husband Clarke, an army lieutenant, in Japan.[20] Mrs. Vaughn said the war became more real for her when German prisoners of war served her in the cafeteria at Fort Lawton. Until that time she, like most American wives, had not come face to face with any aspect of the conflict, and only knew what she read in newspaper articles or saw in movie newsreels. Mrs. Vaughn remembered that required immunization shots made her arms swollen for most of the ocean voyage and that "I was in a dormitory and had to learn to shower with numerous other women. You got over being modest very fast."

The Vaughns' quarters in Japan consisted of two rooms in a Quonset hut—a living area and a bedroom—across the moat from the royal palace.

Clarke was nice enough to get our hut as close as he could to the ladies' bathhouse so I didn't have to walk too far to bathe. It was quite a hike to the men's latrine.

We had no way to cook in our quarters so we ate every meal in a community mess hall with big bottles of salt tablets on the table. I was introduced to peanut butter soup—I never ate peanut butter again. I was a wife who got in on the tail end of "the old Army." I could place an order at the Post Exchange. I would be billed for it, and it would be delivered.

Of course, we did without a lot. There were waiting lists for basics, such as an iron.

Mrs. Eva Ekvall accompanied her husband, a major assigned as military attaché, to Chungking, China. Since her husband's duties carried him over a good part of China, Mrs. Ekvall was fortunate to see much of the country. Traveling by riverboat and jeep, the Ekvalls covered about 7,000 kilometers during a very exciting year.[21]

For Caroline Truitt Giamario, a Civil Service position with the War Department in Korea led to her meeting and marrying a military man.[22] After sailing for twenty-one days from Fort Lewis, Washington, Caroline and seventeen other women arrived at Inchon, Korea. Five of the women, including Caroline, were assigned to the Sixty-first Ordinance Group at ASCOM (Army Service Command) City, which was under Korea Base Command. The only other Americans there were the troops.

Our group was the first group of civilian girls to be sent to Korea. The previous Caucasian women were nurses. We had no time to stop and refresh ourselves or stop and change clothes. We arrived at ASCOM around supper time. Our luggage came the next day—*after* we were met by these freshly shaved men just starved for the sight of Caucasian women. Only two announced they were eligible—Captain Ted Giamario and another man. We were just pooped! I had a black chesterfield coat with a velvet collar just gray with saltwater. It would be three days before we could get cleaned up.

Apparently, Caroline's initial appearance didn't frighten Ted too much, for the couple began dating and were engaged on April 27. Then on August 27, 1947 they were married in the base chapel.

My mother sent my wedding dress. . . . The day of our wedding was a big affair for we were only the second military couple to get married in Korea. Everyone got the day off. . . . The club was set up with champagne, a wedding cake, and a band. Because there weren't any hotels, friends gave us their home for our wedding night. We had another reception at Pusan then took a ferryboat to Japan. Poor Ted. Because he had to have typhoid shots, he was sick the first three days of our honeymoon in Japan. It was the first time I had been in a bathtub since I had gotten to Korea. So while he was sick in bed, I luxuriated in a bathtub.

After the honeymoon, the Giamarios returned to Korea and Japanese-style housing with a big old-fashioned cookstove, which was also used to heat the house. Caroline felt that her experiences in Korea made her more open-minded and helped her later on as a military wife. "I certainly did find adventure by taking that first move overseas," Caroline reiterated. "But I've never been disappointed in my experiences as an army wife. I felt it broadened me very much, especially coming from a small town."

Wives also went to Europe. Beginning in May 1946, converted troop transports carried more than 25,000 women and children to join husbands with the occupation forces in the European theater. The army families were composed of people from six months to sixty years and represented a cross-section of the United States. For many it was a first trip to New York, and most had never traveled east of the Mississippi. The ship, the *Holbrook*, was a transport that was well equipped to handle dependents— from the main dining rooms to the recreation areas to the medical facilities comparable to a sixty-bed hospital.[23] In Bremerhaven, Germany, a warm welcome awaited the dependents:

The two passengers to get off at the first stop received a standing ovation, not only from their waiting husbands but from their traveling companions. Everyone was happy. Passengers roved through the train, lending a helping hand to mothers and their children. . . . As the train commander announced each stop, faces would flush and eyes would sparkle in happy anticipation. Their hearts sang.[24]

International campfollowing became the rule for many Japanese and German women who were war brides of American servicemen. One example is Herta Lund Madsen, who married an American GI in Germany in 1949 and accompanied him throughout his military career.[25] Although her parents were against the match, Herta and her future husband (who was able to obtain permission to marry) persevered. Herta reminisced:

At that time an American serviceman could not marry a German citizen. We were the enemy. So I had to give up my citizenship and become stateless for us to marry. I did this and came with Lee back to America. I worried about being stateless. I remembered reading *The Man Without a Country* and could picture myself drifting on the ocean in a rubber raft from nation to nation. But two years later I got my American citizenship.

Everything was so strange to me. I didn't know how to cook or clean. I had always been in school. I didn't know who had made the beds and cleaned in Germany. Maybe it was my mother or the maid. . . . Once we were at a dinner and the hostess served corn on the cob. I was shocked. We didn't eat corn; we fed it to the pigs. Then everyone took the food in their fingers and began to gnaw the cob. I thought I was among pigs. But I soon adjusted. I was young and adventuresome.

Both Herta and Jeanne Vaughn expressed over and over what many wives said of this time immediately following World War II—that they had never expected to be traveling the world and that, even with many hardships, their journeys were "such an adventure." However, as military wives and their husbands settled into a peacetime army in the United States or an occupation army overseas, little did they realize that renewed conflict was only a few years distant.

CHAPTER EIGHT

A "STANDING ARMY"

Julia Litvack Vean slowly sipped her decaffeinated coffee and hesitated, trying to dredge up from the past memories of her time as a military wife.

> We knew when were married [August 1950] that the country was at war and that Forrie [Forrest] was subject to the draft. All young men were. But I'm not sure I understood what this really meant. It happened so suddenly. I just couldn't believe he was in the army and would soon be on his way to the fighting in Korea. This was what happened to other people.

Like Julia, many American women did not fully comprehend the changes that would occur in their lives when in late June 1950, a flat, unemotional voice reported on the radio, "Today at dawn, North Korean troops crossed the 38th parallel and attacked military forces of the Republic of Korea." How could this announcement affect them? Just five years earlier the United States had won a world war that had brought death and misery to tens of millions. Millions of World War II veterans had been released from active duty or put on reserve status. America was, so they thought, at peace. Soon, however, wives of career military men and draftees would be caught up in a military system that would slowly be forced to accommodate their needs.

THE CHANGES BEGIN

With the onset of the cold war in 1947-48, an atmosphere of
crisis and international commitment developed in the United
States. Because of the uncertainty of the times, the American
aversion to a large standing military force was somewhat set
aside. This meant that from 1940 to 1970 the average American
male spent some time during adolescence or early adulthood in
the service of his country.[1] Although a 1947 War Department
ruling stated, "No man having a wife or child shall be enlisted in
time of peace without special authority from the General Headquarters . . . rule not to apply to soldiers who re-enlist,"[2] military marriages were on the upswing. For many of these young
couples, military life would mean a hand-to-mouth existence.

Since the private sector always offered higher wages than did the
military, both enlisted men and officers worked for lower pay than
their counterparts in civilian jobs. Between 1940 and 1950, for
example, salaries of many civilian professionals increased 100
percent or more while Army officers' salaries rose only by a third.[3]

Even though men were continually entering service through
enlistments, the draft, ROTC, or the military academies, many of
these men felt that a military career did not offer an adequate
standard of living for single or married personnel. In addition to
the low pay scale, lack of housing was a major issue; "lack of
stability for my family caused by frequent moves" was cited by
others.[4] Therefore, many men did not reenlist or resigned their
commissions after completing their required tours of duty. In
1957, official studies showed an exodus of younger officers,
including academy graduates, with a shortage of 28 percent in
the four-to-fourteen-year service group.[5]

Foreseeing potential staffing problems, and because of the
increasing number of dependent families, military planners were
forced to take a hard look at military benefits. Providing adequate
care for dependents would, they felt, help insulate military
personnel from the outside world, provide a sense of security,
foster morale, and encourage an attitude of solidarity. The

changes began in 1942, with rudimentary medical benefits, including some obstetrics, extended to dependents. Post exchanges and commissaries offered goods at discount prices. The military pension system enticed families to consider a twenty- or thirty-year career. On-base housing increased dramatically during the 1950s, and in 1956, the Dependents Medical Care Act led to full health benefits to all military dependents, giving retention of personnel a major shot in the arm. Enlisted pay rose from $870 a year in 1940 to $3,034 in 1960. (This was still nearly $2,000 less than manufacturing workers earned that year.)[6] Family members began to outnumber military personnel as more and more men brought wives into this new pro-family atmosphere. In fact, a 1960 study showed that 84.9 percent of all officers were married, compared to only 69.1 percent of the adult males in the general population.[7] A new responsiblity had been added to the planners for the American military.

THE 38th PARALLEL

Right in the middle of this period of social change and relative peace came the Korean War. War was evolving, and this war was different from World War II as would be the peacekeeping missions, skirmishes, and terrorist conflicts in future decades. Not all of the military was involved in the fighting in Korea. While many military families bade tearful goodbyes to servicemen and waited anxiously for news from the battlefront, many more were involved in peacetime duties stateside and occupation tours in Germany and Japan. Many military people hardly realized a war was going on.

Because the size of the standing army had been reduced after World War II, large numbers of men were brought into service through either the draft or the reserves. Since a great number of these men were married, the military was again faced with the problem of caring for wives and families. The Dependents Assistance Act of 1950 reinstated allowances for enlisted husbands; however, to qualify for this allowance, the men were required "to allot a portion of their basic pay [known as the "Q" allotment] to their wives."[8] Still, this allowance greatly aided the wives, whether they remained in their hometowns or decided to follow their husbands to stateside camps.

Like many Korean War wives, Julia Vean felt that accompanying her enlisted husband Forrest to Fort Leonard Wood, Missouri, was "a short adventure that I shared with him before he was sent to Korea in 1952."[9] Her father drove with her from Colorado to Missouri. "On the way I ran into a cow. The car wasn't damaged, and I don't think the cow was hurt. My father kept asking to drive after that, but I wouldn't let him."

Julia recalled living in a ten-unit motel and paying rent of $25 a week, which "we thought was a fortune." Most of the time she spent by herself or with other wives who had accompanied their husbands as "Forrie only got home late in the evenings and sometimes on weekends." All too soon, of course, her husband of two years was on his way to Korea and she was back home near her parents.

At the beginning of the Korean War, Ginger Sullivan had been told that she would accompany her air force husband to "a house which would be waiting for us in Long Beach."[10] She, their son (who was then two-and-a-half years old), and her husband stayed four or five days in a motel waiting to get into their quarters. "Then, before we could get into our house, Whitney was reassigned to Pittsburgh near Stockton, California. We had to borrow warmer clothing from neighbors, and it was only *ten* days later when Whitney received his orders for Korea." Mrs. Sullivan's odyssey had lasted only two short weeks.

Ginger and other wives watched and waited as the Korean conflict sputtered to a politically unsatisfactory conclusion. However, as in all wars, the wives were simply glad it was over and that their husbands could come home.

During the late 1950s and early 1960s, the country was not engaged in active conflict. However, the cold war still posed a threat, and a substantial part of the American male population still faced mandatory service under the draft. Wives who accompanied these servicemen had some experiences so unusual that they could easily relate them thirty years later.

Marie Long Smith was traveling to a New Jersey post with her army husband who had been drafted in 1955:[11]

> We were pulling a house trailer 'cause we had been told there would be no housing available when we got to his station. Everything that could happen seemed to. We had no gas for cooking in the trailer. Our two children (one eighteen months old and one three weeks old) were very restless. Then we ran out of formula for the baby. Finally, the winds were so high on the Jersey Turnpike that we were put off onto back roads. It seemed like it took us forever to get to the post.

However, the Smiths eventually reached their destination and found they could park their trailer home for only $13.50 per month, a pleasant surprise and an affordable rent. "And best of all," Marie recalled, "the site came with a beautiful view of the ocean right below us." For other military wives of this period, Marie's experience must seem very similar to their own.

Some experiences left a bitter taste, however. Even with many American males having served in the military (48.5 percent of the 49.5 million employed American males in 1970 were veterans),[12] public sentiment toward those in uniform was not always positive. To many civilians, military people were merely vagabonds, here today and gone tomorrow, and necessary only because United States policy in the second half of the twentieth century was to maintain a large standing force. The military community was for many "a kind of foreign settlement . . . relations [with those outside were] uneasy and even exploitative."[13] Civilians were hesitant to rent them housing; mothers warned their children "not to play with the army kids;" business and industry discriminated against the military wife in hiring.

Ginger Sullivan recalled a particularly humiliating situation. Preparing alone for a move to Bermuda (after the Korean War), she wanted assurance that the family's household goods would be safely handled. At the office of the moving company she was asked, "What could a military wife have that would be of any value?" She still remembered the stinging hurt thirty years later, although this may have been one of the mild rebuffs that military wives took.

A RETURN TO GENTILITY

The halcyon years between the end of the Korean War and the escalation of the Vietnam conflict saw the military wife caught up in the pre-World War II traditions of the regular army. A good military wife who was working to help promote her husband would call on senior officers' wives, volunteer for charitable activities, and attend a round of teas, coffees and luncheons. All were expected duties and the wives fulfilled them admirably.

One navy wife recalled her phone ringing on a Sunday afternoon in Coronado, California:

> It was Mrs. Captain's wife who said she and her husband would like to pay a return call on us, and they would be there in fifteen minutes. None of our nice things had arrived yet; my husband was scheduled to leave for Mexico the next day; I had a cold. I have never seen my husband move so fast.

The wife remembered that she was quite concerned because they didn't have a calling card tray, the traditional silver salver, and had to use a soup plate.

> The captain and his wife came in, couldn't have been nicer. She had white gloves, all according to protocol. I offered them hors d'oeuvres and cocktails. We were just getting comfortable when she picked up her gloves and put them in her lap. Her husband turned to my husband and in mid-sentence said that they would have to go. She had given him the signal. They had stayed the required twenty minutes; that was it! Military protocol had been satisfied.

Because of the increasing number of military families in the cold war era, the military attempted to socialize families into "a modified version of the military model, anticipating their role as a kind of special support system."[14] Wives were told, for example, that the army, like the navy, was "making a bid for civilian favor. It is important that we merit the respect of taxpayers and that all army wives do their utmost in promoting cordial relations."[15] The feeling existed that the esteem, respect, and dignity given to marriage by wives could be extended "to the integrity and justice of the boundless frontier of democracy our country represents."[16]

Following in this vein, a series of books and pamphlets emphasizing the full-time support of the military man were made available to the wives of both enlisted men and officers. Both *The Army Wife* (by Nancy Shea) and *The Navy Wife* (by Shea and Anne Briscoe Pye) stressed that homemaking was a full-time job, that caring for children was the job for which each wife was designed, and that the wife should not work outside the home if this would interfere with her home responsibilities. Outlines showed the specific duties of the good military wife. For the enlisted wife these were (1) to make a congenial home, (2) to rear a family of which he will be proud, and (3) to strengthen her husband's morale. It was then emphasized that "your whole scheme of life revolves around your husband, your children, and a happy home." In addition to the above duties, the NCO's wife was cautioned to set a good example for the younger soldiers' wives, join the NCO Wives' Club, and assist the unit commander's wife whenever necessary.[17] Rules were enunciated for even the most basic social graces. Enlisted wives were admonished: "Don't comb your hair, blow your nose or use a toothpick in a restaurant or at the dining table."[18]

Officers' wives also were told what was expected of them, including when to wear white gloves, a hat, or a formal gown. The junior officer's wife had to assume that the three basic duties, as outlined for the enlisted wife, would be "foremost in your life." In addition she was told to be eager and interested, take an active interest in company or unit programs, and join in volunteer work. The senior wife in addition had many social necessities, such as calling on the bride or newcomer; promoting morale and spirit through a series of open houses, picnics, or sporting events; and arranging coffees or teas with the Officers' Wives' Club where any "company family" business could be taken care of.[19] The officer and his wife were once again the aristocracy of the traditional military.

These relatively untroubled years came to an end, however, as the conflict in Vietnam escalated into a full-scale war. Once again, men were on the move to places where the wives could not go.

VIETNAM REMEMBERED

The Vietnam conflict brought a new type of tour. For most men, the tour of duty was only twelve months, rather than for the duration of hostilities as in World War II and many times in Korea. There was also a new type of "campfollowing." As in Korea, those women whose husbands were stationed stateside or in Europe, the Mideast, and parts of Asia not directly involved in the war continued to accompany husbands to bases around the country and overseas. The husbands of some wives who were at bases in the Pacific were drawn into the conflict, flying missions over Vietnam and then returning to the routine of a "peacetime" base. The Sullivans were stationed on Guam at that time, and Ginger remembered anxious moments as her husband, then a lieutenant colonel, flew in and out of Vietnam.

However, most wives with career or draftee husbands in Southeast Asia could only meet their husbands for a week or two at various rest and recreation (R & R) sites throughout the world. Many did this, spending a brief week reunited in Honolulu or rarely in the Philippines, Japan, Australia, or Thailand. The men had their jobs and the women were again left behind to cope with fear, loneliness, and the day-to-day responsibility of maintaining a home.

One air force officer's wife experienced firsthand the stress the war caused on families that were split apart. Anne told of witnessing many divorces of other wives as she struggled to keep her marriage intact. She and her husband Sam were married when he was civilian—a student with his entry deferred until the end of the semester. He joined the air force on a delayed enlistment plan because he had not completed his degree. Therefore, he went to basic training as an enlisted man and then continued immediately on to officer training. For Anne it was a completely different world:

> There were a lot of separations at first. He went through a year of pilot training which was extremely stressful. . . . There was an enormous time pressure. Our day began at 5 A.M. He studied until midnight to get all the stuff done. He might as well have been a bachelor for there was no time for me or the family—even on the weekend. Incredible! One of the reasons they maintained the schedule was to weed out those who could not take stress.
>
> Stress! I had my baby by myself. Then we were moved. I knew absolutely no one. No glimmer of who to have as a baby-sitter, no friends. He began to fly tankers in the Young Tiger missions accompanying B-52s to Thailand, Okinawa, the Philippines, and Taiwan. He would be gone for three months, home for one month, gone for two. This went on for more than two years. Vietnam was rough for we always wondered what was happening.

Particularly stressful to Anne was trying to follow housing regulations while living alone on-base during the months her husband was in Southeast Asia.

> We had a base commander who was extremely picky about lawns. I had to buy an electric mower and edger and had to pass inspection. People would get "tickets" for getting grass in the cracks in their sidewalks and get reported to the base

commander. When the husband got back from his trip to
Vietnam, he'd get a report. You'd have to get a screwdriver
to pry the grass out. I am not kidding! So on one hand was
the stress of not knowing if your husband was still alive; on
the other it was stress from the pickiness of manicuring your
lawn.

Joan Brennan McDavid had three children and was expecting
a fourth when her husband Jim, a marine captain, received orders
to Vietnam.[20] He took his family from Camp Pendleton in
California to Columbia, South Carolina, near his parents, and
then left in January. The baby was due in March, and his parents
were scheduled to help out when Joan went to the hospital. But
shortly before the baby was due, both of Jim's parents had to be
hospitalized. Fortunately, for Joan, her sister was able to come
from Pennsylvania and help out. Joan remembered that one of
her neighbors was kind enough to go the airport at 4 A.M. to meet
the sister, as Joan was already in labor.

The McDavid's oldest son was in second grade at the time, old
enough to realize that his father was in Vietnam, to miss his
companionship, and to realize the danger. The boy had become
more reserved after his father left, less willing to talk with Joan
or voice his fears. She became particularly aware of her son's
concern over the separation when she overheard one of the boy's
friends inquire, "How's your dad?"

"Oh, he's fine," the boy replied quickly and then added, "He's
not dead yet."

Monday through Friday in the late evenings Joan would gather
the children together for a special project in their home. Then
dinner would follow immediately.

I felt this would keep their minds occupied and they would
not have to see the other fathers coming home from work
when they knew their father could not do so. I hoped this
would keep their thoughts off the war and off his not being
at home with them.

For another wife, however, it was far worse because her husband was shot down in Vietnam. Carol was comfortably settled in a rental home near a base when her husband left for a mission over Vietnam. She thought she was lucky to be established near a base. If there was room, some bases allowed the prisoner of war (POW) and missing in action (MIA) wives to remain. Other wives she knew were asked to move out when their husbands were reported missing in action. "If you were established at a base and were allowed to stay, it really was a help for there was a camaraderie established. It was really difficult for the wife to move and try to reconnect," Carol noted. Later she and the wives of other MIAs banded together.

> There came a time when we tried to organize. The services were reluctant to give much information—even to other wives. The navy wives finally got the names and addresses and started a grass roots organization. Other wives we found were not able to get their husbands' paychecks. I was lucky for I did.
>
> My husband volunteered for Vietnam. He left in January 1968 and was shot down in April. For twenty months I didn't hear anything. I made friends and they kept me busy. One would call and say that we were going to the beach and to get my fishing pole. Life had to go on. I kept hoping that he was alive. After twenty months I got word he had been taken prisoner. He was a POW for five years; he came home in 1973.
>
> During the time he was in prison, little by little we became an MIA family. We started collecting signatures and began a letter-writing campaign. We had to fight for everything we got, even though we were military and had a good background. Once we asked the wives' club for assistance with postage for a letter-writing campaign. The base commander questioned our request. We had to fight for even getting a table in front of the commissary to collect petitions. . . . Vietnam was not a popular war.

Vietnam was not a popular war, and for many of the military wives with husbands in Southeast Asia the memories are particularly bitter ones. Even if their husbands were not directly involved in the war, they were constantly made aware that many citizens did not support the United States' involvement. Military men were no longer viewed by many as "good guys." For the wives as well as the men it was a stressful period.

"The Vietnam War killed the romanticism of war," explained Julie Farnsworth,[21] a young army wife who married in the post-Vietnam era.

> In World War II, it was romantic; we were out to fight Nazi Germany and free the people. The women were working to free the men to fight. My father and brother were in Vietnam. My father was a lieutenant colonel and my brother an infantryman. We felt that if anyone was going to be killed it would have been father. I remember packing cookies with my mother. My brother was missing for a period of time. He was wounded, and we were afraid he'd lose a leg. That's when war ceases to be a John Wayne movie.

One woman who went to Vietnam as a Red Cross recreation director experienced the stress alluded to by Vietnam wives. She told of coming back to Washington to recruit and train new workers.

> It was a very difficult time. On one hand, in Vietnam, when I worked in the hospital, it was not so much death that bothered me as the maiming, the loss of sight, the disfiguring of so many young American men. Then to come back to Washington, where at first everything seemed so normal and life just kept going on, it was like stepping back into a foreign world as opposed to being a foreign world where I had been. It was very strange. Then with the peace riots on top of that, it was so very confusing emotionally and extremely stressful. . . . It was a strange kind of situation for the men to be

so rejected and unaccepted after giving so much of them-selves, even the ones who survived uninjured.

Back in the states, wives of these men were experiencing rejection also. Joan McDavid recalled that while many of the people she met in Columbia, South Carolina, were most helpful and friendly, several times she had prowlers or peeping Toms around her home. The most frightening incident involved the mail.

There was a bomb—a sort of Molotov cocktail—put into the mailbox next door to my house. It exploded when no one was near the box, so no one was hurt. But the next morning a retired marine colonel who lived across the street from me came over and said, "I don't want to alarm you, Joan, but I think that bomb was meant for your box."

The memories for most wives are mixed. When Joan and her four children went to the airport to meet Jim on his return from overseas, the oldest son told several other waiting people that his daddy was coming home from Vietnam. "Several of the men in the waiting area asked me if it would be okay if they stayed around and shook his hand," Joan recalled. It made me feel very good. (Nearly ten years later, Jim told Joan that while flying in uniform from Atlanta to Columbia, a young woman had asked him where he was coming from. When he replied "Vietnam," she spit on him and moved to another seat on the plane.)

Judith Smith Lott[22] also recalled how she and her husband were received when they returned to their hometown in Florida.

We were young and proud of the fact that he was in the army. He also felt that it was his duty to go to Vietnam. But when we got back home where we had always lived prior to his going in the military, where we had grown up and gone to school, almost all of our friends would have nothing to do with us. He had played in a band with some of the guys, but they avoided him also. In fact, if we called most people that we had known before, they either gave us some excuse why they couldn't see us or only talked very briefly with us. It really hurt.

Several wives mentioned that, in order to forestall possible harassment, military men in the Boston area were cautioned against wearing their uniforms off-base. Faith Dix, the mother of a Vietnam Congressional Medal of Honor winner and a former military wife herself, remembered how sad she felt when several people whom she had thought to be close friends wrote or telephoned negative comments. "Many of them said the most insulting things. Told me that he was a murderer. Here he had received the highest military honor America can give, and it was without doubt the worst time of my life."[23]

Mildred Schwab Martinez also recalled a distressing incident during the time she was with her husband at an Army base in Indiana.

The people there didn't like us, didn't like the military people. They were not happy about the United States being in Vietnam. I remember a 4th of July parade where the bystanders threw eggs on the army men as they marched in the parade. It was very humiliating for the wives and for the men.[24]

"What was hardest for me," said one army wife, "was having to deal with the fact that my husband was gone and that no one I knew really cared. It's as if Vietnam was a void that swallowed all of them."

When the men did return from Southeast Asia, for many it was not a simple homecoming. The wives and the children had changed—had most times become quite capable and independent. Many of the veterans had considerable difficulty adjusting to changes in American culture and to the hostile attitudes of some American civilians. Often their reactions would be anger, grief, or depression. Men were diagnosed as having post-traumatic stress disorder (PTSD), and some estimates of the number of veterans who would need psychiatric help reached 1.5 million.[25] Still, the military family survived and moved forward to face the end of the draft and the proposed all-volunteer force.

AFTER 'NAM

Shortly, changes which had their roots in the latter part of the 1960s became more evident. The end of the draft and the transition (1971-73) to an all-volunteer military was a major transformation and, some say, dissolved the feelings of solidarity so encouraged in the earlier military. The number of wives did not decrease though; by 1975, more than half of all army personnel were married, with similar figures for the other armed forces. Wives were a fixture of military life, but many were not altogether happy with the status quo.

Advocates of the Equal Rights Amendment and the women's movement challenged women to seek fulfillment outside of their traditional roles and to demand a better world for themselves and their families. No longer were all military wives content to accept a lifestyle consisting many times of a salary lower than that of comparable civilians, substandard housing, poor dependent schools, inequality in job opportunities, and loneliness. Because of this, both outside institutions and the military took a greater interest in the service family. Particularly in the late 1970s and early 1980s, the lifestyle of the military spouse came under scrutiny as study after study was funded to help understand the needs of the military families.

CHAPTER NINE

OH, WHAT AN ADVENTURE

Many wives call their time in the military the "glory years." These were the years when they were young, resilient, and eager for change, were excited by the travel and the adventure of being a citizen of the world, and anxious to add their personality to the changing scene. A military career is intense—lasting less than twenty years for some, for others up to thirty—filled with sharp peaks and devastating lows, hell to live through but glorious to recount.

How these days are viewed depends on personal experience. For some women bitterness and anger permeate any conversation about the military. They recall men who were killed or maimed physically or psychologically by war. Many complain about being left to rear children and grow old alone.

Others chafe under the restrictions of the caste system that has separated officers from enlisted for the entire history of the military. As one enlisted wife explained, "At the Air Force Academy there are two *very* separate housing areas. One, Douglas (Doug) Valley is known as Smug Valley. The other area, Pine Valley, is laughingly called Swine Valley. It doesn't take a genius to discern in which section the officers live."

Some dwell on the security of guaranteed retirement benefits, which can range from $15,000 a year for a senior chief with over twenty years to $45,000 for a retired colonel. Other women tell of their rich experiences, journeying around the world, an adventure fueled by a positive state of mind and the perception that they had a good life in spite of the continual hardships. They experienced a sense of bonding from the military community as well as a sisterhood that bridged the times alone and helped when tragedy or illness struck. These women say that the very act of being a military wife starts a lifelong period of learning, many times converting a small-town girl into a highly polished, worldly-wise, well-traveled and versatile woman who is able to cope and survive. As military wives, these women outgrew the provincial environment they left—whether it was Mainline Philadelphia or a small town in the Deep South—and transformed themselves as they influenced those they met in their travels.

As dependents of a large, impersonal bureaucracy that had traditionally viewed wives as excess baggage, the needs of these women were long relegated to the backwaters of military concern. With the proportion of married personnel reaching over 60 percent in the 1970s and 1980s and discontent among families being cited as a major cause for men leaving the service, the armed forces saw the necessity of investigating the key roll that wives play in the continuity of the nation's military.

UNDER THE MICROSCOPE

For over 100 years the world of the American military wife had remained hidden beneath the romance and tradition of her military husband. Mainly viewed as a nuisance by the military men of the Revolutionary War, she won grudging acceptance for her nursing skills in the Civil War and for her survival ability on the frontier. Gradually, in the twentieth century, the military granted her the status of "dependent wife." Still, she existed only in the background—a helpmate, a volunteer, a silent partner whose needs, wishes, and problems remained hidden.

However, in order to keep the man in the military, the life of the military wife and family was placed under a microscope by clinical investigators in what was one of the first important studies funded by the Department of Defense (DOD) on the effects of the military lifestyle on families. In the ensuing years, such studies proliferated: The Submariners' Wives Syndrome; Separation Reactions of Married Women; The Maritime Marriage: A Form of Episodic Monogamy; The WESTPAC Widow; and Common Psychological Syndromes of the Army Wife. Military wives were finding their place in the professional journals next to the Vietnam veterans and the prisoners of war.

WHAT SOME OF THE STUDIES SHOW

One of the early studies was *Families Under Stress, The Adjustment to the Crises of War, Separation and Reunion*. Author Reuben Hill identified the external threat of dismemberment, or separation, common to every family when the man was called to war—even a war as "popular" as World War II in which all Americans were encouraged to do their patriotic best to help the war effort.[1] In World War II, the wives and families sent their men to war with a sense of participation in a great cause in which they played a vital part. Even the Korean conflict was generally viewed as necessary to defend democracy against the encroachment of communism. As devastating as these two wars were to the waiting wives, even more devastating was the unpopular war of Vietnam. Like those before them, Vietnam wives faced the emptiness of separation and survival with the added burden of living in communities that not only did not understand their husbands' roles but were not supportive.

Hill noted that the crises coming from without the family, viewed as being beyond their control, were different from the crises arising out of interpersonal relations within the family.[2] What seems to remain the same in subsequent studies is that people in a military family are often isolated from their extended family, but without the support of an adequate substitute. As one wife recently put it as she reflected on her life, "In the isolation of military living, friends become our family."

Hill stressed that to weather the storms of war, families had to have good coping skills:

Good adjustment to separation involved closing of ranks, shifting of responsibilities and activities of the father to other members, continuing the family outings, maintaining husband-wife and father-child relationships by correspondence and visits, utilizing the resources of friends, relatives and neighbors, and carrying on plans for the reunion.[3]

Hill noted that, just as adjustment was needed during separation, homecoming required a readjustment. The father's return required realigning the power and authority in the home, renewing intimacies between husband and wife, resuming father-child ties, replanning family labor and recreational activities, and reworking and putting into action plans made before and during separation.[4] Advice from this early study would greatly benefit wives waiting to greet Vietnam veterans twenty-five years later.

The studies of the military family were not concerned solely with wartime effects. Some twenty years later, three studies looked at the crisis of separation not from that of a man plucked out of a family to fight a war but to maintain the cold war defense system in a nuclear submarine. These important studies were separately authored by Richard A. Isay, M.D.; Chester A. Pearlman, Jr., M.D.; and the Reverend Robert W. Bermudes. Each study was based on research involving wives of submariners stationed at Groton, Connecticut, the site of the navy's Submarine Training Center. Homeport for some 5,100 navy families, the men were stationed aboard one of three types of submarines: Fleet Ballistic Missile (FBM) submarine, nuclear-powered fast attack submarines, or the older, conventional diesel submarines.

By the time of Isay's study, the FBM submarines, first launched in 1960, had been operating for nine years. Each submarine has two crews, a Blue and a Gold, permitting the boat to operate more efficiently year round, with the exception of time in port to refit and restock. The system may have been more effective from the navy's point of view, but as the years passed it was realized that the cycle of departures and homecomings caused serious problems for the wife, husband, and marriage. Isay termed it the "submariners' wives syndrome," and explained that, on the average, submariners spent three months on sea patrol and three months on shore duty for a total of six patrols. This three-year cycle might be repeated a number of times at varying intervals during the submariner's career.

Other men at the base, on conventional submarines, were at sea for irregular periods averaging from seven to nine months of the year, even longer than the men on Polaris submarines. "The Submarine Base, then, may be viewed as a unique culture in which the majority of men have agreed to be away from their families for extensive periods of time with the acquiescence of their wives, who are partners in this unusual marital situation."[5]

In Pearlman's study, it was noted that "no matter how often the experience [of separation] was repeated, each separation was a psychological crisis. . . . Each patient showed the same successive phases of protest against acceptance of the separation, despair and detachment. . . ."[6] The cycle included feelings of increasing tension and the question, "Why does he really have to go?" Next was a tearful period in which the patient felt, "I'll never live through three months without him." This was followed by an attitude of not caring if he ever returned. Pearlman also noted that "each reunion evoked a converse pattern of impulses to punish the husband for having been away. . . ." Each of these reactions would last about three to four weeks with this separation–reunion sequence involving some six to eight weeks of psychological turmoil every six months. Pearlman concluded that "the experience of the great majority of submariners' wives has clearly indicated that successful adaptation to the separation crisis requires the capacity to be alone."[7]

This pattern of emotions was seen in a different light by Reverend Bermudes, who wondered if there was some degree of correlation between the submarine wives' emotional highs and lows and the responses to grief normally observed when someone loses a loved one through death. From his study, Bermudes mapped out a recommendation of a healing ministry to the repeatedly grief-stricken.[8]

In 1977, based on tests she administered in a pilot study of 48 submariners' wives, Alice Ivey Snyder, Ph.D. found evidence to support the belief

that separation of spouse was perceived as a stressful life event by these women . . . physical illnesses of the women do tend to follow the cycle of separation and reunion and that available medical facilities are not completely equipped to deal with the physical and psychological implications of this correlation. It was also found that marital separation does not carry the same connotation as for a civilian population. If the wife is unhappy with the military pressures on her life, studies show that her attitude influences her husband's attitude and ultimately his career.[9]

In addition to the above, the DOD has funded a multitude of studies and papers dealing with all aspects of the military family. One such study, conducted by Major Gerald F. Murray (USAF), was on the link between retention of officers and the type of jobs their wives have. Murray analyzed responses from 34,000 questionnaires completed by military families. It was found that if a wife had a job that paid well, her officer-husband was more likely to remain in the military.[10]

Mario R. Schwabe and Florence W. Kaslow reported on violence in the military family. In addition to quoting extensively from authorities in the civilian as well as the military world, the authors concluded:

Many characteristics of military life affect the risk for violence. Perhaps the most significant is the removal of the military family, usually young and inexperienced, from the support systems of the extended family and family friends. . . . Frequently, military couples have to live in quarters assigned according to rank. Their neighbors, therefore, are also young people with little more experience in marriage and parenting than they have.[11]

It would be impossible to cite all of the studies and papers which have poured forth over the last few years. However, their topics point to the changing world of the military family, the challenges of military family life, and the trends in recent military family patterns.

Through all of the research, the branches of the armed forces realized that although it was the man who was in the military, it was the wife who determined how successful his career would be. And there were an increasing number of bright young officers and highly trained enlisted men who were giving up military careers after serving only one term because their families were suffering. Edna J. Hunter, perhaps one of the most prolific writer/researchers in the field of the military family, commented,

> Ironically, although it has been found that family support, particularly that from the wife, is one of the most important factors influencing a military man's performance on the job, wives have, until recently, been viewed as "dependents," whose own needs were often ignored by the organization in which she found herself firmly entrenched.[12]

The military command could no longer ignore the reciprocal influences which work-family interactions had on the system as a whole.

As a result of the many studies and articles documenting the military family's problems, a number of programs were instituted to try to make life more rewarding, for both military personnel and their spouses. Included in these were the Department of Defense Family Advocacy Program, which was mandated in 1981 to create servicewide programs for the identification and prevention of spouse and child abuse; the Military Family Act of 1985, which provided base commanders the option of allowing Family Day Care Homes programs to function on base; and Spouse Employment Centers (1982), designed to aid military spouses in obtaining information about employment opportunities in specific locations.

However, perhaps the most beneficial service provided by the military is the Family Support Center, which acts as a base-level advocate for military personnel and family members. On most military sites, depending on funding and available staff, these centers are the focal points for information and referral to both on-base and off-base helping agencies. Professional counseling is available, either at the base or on a referral basis in the community, for help with marriage and financial problems, job-search techniques, or classes in areas such as assertiveness training, communicating, parenting, stress management and a host of others. In addition, the Family Services program, administered by the Family Support Center and staffed mostly by volunteers, assists families in various ways. On many bases an Airman's Closet, stocked with items donated by military families, help alleviate hardships to E-4s and below with dependents. On the birth of a child, a complimentary layette is given to E-4s and below. Assistance is provided for families during moves or during extended periods of separation when a service member is on unaccompanied overseas tours. Current information is also provided to spouses about benefits to which they are entitled.

However, with all of these services, wives still speak highly of the help they get from each other. The concept of bonding and the "sisterhood" of military wives (that closeness and sharing of both happiness and hardship which ran as a thread through the lives of the frontier military wives) is emphasized again and again by today's modern military spouses.

THE SISTERHOOD

Harriet Weissman exudes comfort and caring as she tells of the changes she has undergone and of the bonds she has made as a result of her thirty-five years of marriage to a navy man who retired as a captain.[13]

> I do not have a college degree, so my learning came from meeting different people from all walks of life—and I soaked

it up. I grew up in New York and never ventured out of the state all of those years. And growing up a Jew meant I had a very narrow and sheltered viewpoint. Meeting people of all different faiths and cultures, as I did as a navy wife, broadens you unbelievably; you learn to accept people from all backgrounds. I notice the difference even more when we go back home to visit. I feel like I'm back in the dark ages. My cousins in New York still have the same parochial, narrow viewpoint. With the military moving you every two to three years, you meet new groups of people and you are forced to reach out to make friends. . . . Navy life has definitely broadened me.

Harriet Weissman is the kind of woman who turns a disadvantage into an advantage. Her husband was sent to Japan during a time when wives were encouraged to stay home. She packed up their four children, arranged passage on an army transport ship to Japan, and endured the seasickness to spend six weeks with her husband. Another wife might have asked, "Was it worth it?" For Harriet it was

a romantic six weeks, like a rendezvous with this handsome man. We didn't have a phone; we didn't know when we'd see each other, so we had these signals we'd use—a card posted on the officers' club bulletin board that said: "See you at _____." Then I'd know he'd be home that night.

When you are a military wife, you have to be able to roll with the punches. If the wife is not happy being a service wife, then that man's career is not going anywhere and he might as well get out of the service. You survive, with a lot of humor and a lot of support from the other wives, the being alone, the responsibilities of children and house. Ten minutes after my husband Marv's plane was in the air we organized a bowling team, a bridge group, a theater party—whatever was needed to keep our morale up.

When there were problems, the CO's [commanding officer's] wife would filter that information down to the women, and we would help. We had seven first babies born while the husbands were away, so those of us who had second or third children became the focal point for these new mothers. We became family to them, and we remain in touch with them over the years. When you help someone raise a child for six months, you become like a sister or mother to them. In our squadron of thirty, the wives of the fourteen men on the crew became like family because in the air their job could be a matter of life or death.

Many women cited this sense of belonging to a larger family: a family which pulled together when sickness or tragedy struck. There are so many stories that could have been told of military communities that banded together to help just as would be expected in small-town America. One story in particular typifies the military experience.

"I never realized the natural family support system functioning within the Navy until my husband underwent very serious surgery," noted Mary Beth Mills.[14] "Without my asking, there were at least two people with me during the eleven-hour wait while he was in surgery—from the chaplain, to the chaplain's wife, to the ship's doctor, to a shipmate."

Mrs. Mills, who was previously married to a civilian, made the comparison between a crisis then (when she waited alone during a life-threatening surgery on her four-year-old daughter, found sitters for her healthy children, and managed the home by herself) and the support of navy wives. "What a difference! This extended family, to me, is the greatest benefit of all."

This bonding is especially noted among wives of crew members, whether it be of an airplane or a submarine. These women are thrown together for extended periods of time. When the men are deployed, the wives have a ready-made social community.

Sandra Paige[15] recalled:

We were stationed at a base in northern Maine. A pilot hopped a flight on a fighter; it crashed. In that tragedy was my first experience with the magnificence of a military community. Wives started a telephone tree to organize cooking meals for the widow. Every morning there was someone at her door with breakfast breads and eggs. For three weeks, every meal was delivered so she didn't have to cook or do dishes.

It may have been that experience that led Sandra Paige to the job she held as director of an Air Force Family Support Center. In an official capacity, she headed a team of people that interfaced with the Hickam Air Force Base community and its needs.

MORE THAN A TOURIST

While most military wives cite travel as one of the "perks," reassignment orders bring much more than a tourist view of a new area. Being a military wife means not just visiting various bases and cities in the United States and overseas, but actually living there, whether you like the place or not, for an extended time. This involves getting to know the people and the customs of the area or country. A move brings mixed feelings—sadness at leaving and the thrill of a new challenge.

Roberta (Bobbie) Junge,[16] who grew up in a small town near Pittsburgh, felt that travel was one of the high points of being a military wife. She even included her very first move to the South—with a dose of humor.

You have to understand that I grew up not knowing anything about the military. I left a very secure, very social, outgoing environment with family and classmates. Well, when Bernie and I got married, he was an E-2 [junior enlisted] in the air force and we moved immediately to downtown Dudley, North Carolina, right outside Seymour Johnson. [Rolling her eyes for emphasis, Bobbie stressed the 'Dud' in Dudley.] It was my first exposure to people from the South, the way they did things and the way they talked. I would sit in amazement at the slower pace. It was a whole different lifestyle.

All of a sudden I became a recluse. We rented a trailer, had one car which Bernie took to work. I had no friends, no one to sit and have coffee with, no one to have over for dinner, nothing in common with other wives. I read more in that first year than I ever had. But we adjusted.

The Junge's next move was to Germany, which Bobbie liked a great deal. "There was such a camaraderie; the German people were so welcoming." The Junges lived in half of a house with landlords who were willing to teach Bobbie about their culture. Bobbie recalled that there were a number of military wives who wouldn't attempt to get their driving licenses, who wouldn't go anywhere. However, Bobbie found a great deal of excitement in Europe:

It was exciting for me being a small-town girl, walking on the Champs-Elysées, seeing the Mona Lisa, standing outside the gates at Buckingham Palace, spending Christmas in Munich, which was like experiencing Hansel and Gretel. My husband and I walked from Switzerland to Austria.

In one sense it was hard for us because the dollar was fluctuating so much, and we had to live within our means, but I found a job and that helped. Every weekend we toured somewhere because we wanted to see everything and learn everything we could. For me it was fascinating to talk to older German people about the war. I stood at Dachau and saw in my mind what happened.

Jean Wood is another small-town girl who never dreamed of all of the places she would see nor of the changes the army would bring into her life. She and her husband Roy were married in their senior year in college. He finished his degree six months before her, was commissioned into the army, and was sent to language school prior to going to Italy. She completed her degree at Berkeley and joined him at the language school, where she took classes offered for the wives in "language and deportment as an officer's wife."[17]

> It was at the school that I learned how really green I was. Some of the senior officers' wives took me shopping and helped me polish up the way I dressed. Through them, I entered into a different world. I learned the language along with Roy, as well as a little about Italian art, history, and culture in the wives' courses.

The Woods' first assignment was overseas. They lived in a duplex with an Italian couple who became like grandparents to the two children Jean bore there. Being overseas meant living without all of the luxuries they had considered so necessary in the states.

> We did without electricity, making do with less light, not using a dishwasher or dryer because the cost of electricity was prohibitive. I did diapers by hand with an old wringer-washer and used a pole with a couple of boards in place of the closet we never had. Even though we lived on the economy, we were still better off than the locals.
>
> The army offered me changes. I never would have thought of being able to travel to Europe or Asia. I made every tour an adventure. We chose to stay in Italy because . . . it was relatively free of drugs. We were in Naples from 1975 to 1979, and the children made friends that they still fly clear across the states to see. In Italy I often had one to six kids in my house, and the parents knew you would care for them. It was like having an extended family. It was a fabulous experience for the children that I don't think we could have duplicated here in the U.S.

As Bobbie Junge and many other wives have said, it is attitude that makes the difference in how life is perceived. This was true for all military wives. When Elizabeth Custer wrote of the prairies rife with wildflowers, she was for the moment choosing to ignore the drabness of her spartan quarters. When Elizabeth Helmick told of voyages to the Philippines or Alaska, she dwelled on the wondrous sights, not the weeks of seasickness or the fear of traveling alone. When today's wife writes home of the "paradise" known as Hawaii, she seldom complains about the high cost of living or inadequate housing.

While these military wives come from different periods in history, their campfollowing episodes have a similar beginning and ending. Certainly, over the past 200 years, the military lifestyle has changed drastically. Muskets have given way to rocket launchers, the cavalry has become mechanized, and a fledgling World War I air corps has its sights set on space. The role of the military man has become ever more challenging in this technological age. However, as this brief history has shown, the military wife's role is basically the same today as it was when Elizabeth Custer crossed the frontier or when Elizabeth Helmick sailed to the Philippines. She is expected to be an uncomplaining helpmate, lover, mother, social butterfly, and volunteer extraordinaire. She must always be aware that the military comes first. When her husband gets orders, her campfollowing begins.

NOTES

CHAPTER 1

1. William W. Fowler, *Women on the American Frontier* (Hartford, Conn.: S.S. Scranton, 1878), 136.

2. Sally Smith Booth, *The Women of '76* (New York: Hastings House, 1973), 181.

3. William Addleman Ganoe, *The History of the United States Army* (New York: D. Appleton-Century Company, 1942), 17.

4. Ganoe, 41.

5. John Elting (Col. U.S. Army, Retired), *American Army Life* (New York: Charles Scribner's Sons, 1982), 25.

6. Page Smith, *A New Age Now Begins*, vol. 2 (New York: McGraw-Hill, 1976), 1811.

7. Smith, 1602.

8. Linda Grant DePauw, *Founding Mothers* (Boston: Houghton Mifflin, 1975), 182.

9. Smith, 1602.

10. Frank Donovan, *The George Washington Papers* (New York: Dodd, Mead, 1964), 144, 153, 169.

11. DePauw, 183–84.

12. Anne Hollingsworth Wharton, *Colonial Days and Dames* (Philadelphia: J.B. Lippincott, 1895), 97.

13. Christopher Ward, *The War of the Revolution*, vol. 2, John Richard Aiden, ed., (New York: Macmillan, 1952), 799.

14. Ward, 721.

15. DePauw, 184.

16. Mary Ormsbee Whitton, *These Were the Women, USA 1776-1860* (New York: Random House, 1954), 6.

17. Burke Davis, *George Washington and the American Revolution* (New York: Random House, 1975), 56.

18. Paul Engle, *Women in the American Revolution* (Chicago: Follett, 1976), 252.

19. Alice Curtis Desmond, *Martha Washington, Our First Lady* (New York: Dodd, Mead, 1976), 165.

20. Beverly Utley, "Women of the Revolution," in *The Uncommon Soldier of the Revolution* (Philadelphia: Eastern Acorn Press, 1986, with permission of the original publisher, Historical Times, Harrisburg), 10.

21. Engle, 223.

22. Booth, 162.

23. Engle, 222.

24. Desmond, 167.

25. Donovan, 132.

26. Elizabeth F. Ellet, *The Women of the American Revolution*, vol. 2, 4th ed. (New York: Haskell House, 1969), 17.

27. Desmond, 160–61.

28. Booth, 165.

29. Desmond, 154.

30. Desmond, 166.

31. Whitton, 6.

32. Booth, 161.

33. Desmond, 145–46.

34. Thomas Fleming, *1776, Year of Illusion* (New York: W.W. Norton, 1975), 55.

35. Georth Athan Bellias, ed., *George Washington's Generals* (New York: William Morrow, 1964), 242–43.

36. Bellias, 243.

37. George F. Scheer and Hugh F. Rankin, *Rebels and Redcoats* (New York: World Publishing, 1957), 310.

38. Bellias, 120.

39. Desmond, 162.

40. Scheer, 310.

41. David J. Harkness, "Heroines of the American Revolution," *University of Tennessee Newsletter*, 40, no. 1 (February, 1961): 2.

42. Scheer, 358.

43. Desmond, 191.

44. Bellias, 81.

45. Booth, 181.

46. Lynn Montross, *The Story of the Continental Army, 1775-1783* (New York: Barnes & Noble, 1952), 143.

47. Davis, 213.

48. Booth, 183.

49. Booth, 181–82.

50. Booth, 173–74.

51. Elizabeth Evans, *Weathering the Storm* (New York: Charles Scribner & Sons, 1975), 11.

52. John Laffin, *Women in Battle* (London: Abelard-Schuman, 1967), 104.

53. Booth, 174.

54. Booth, 98–99; DePauw, 189.

55. Booth, 98–99.

56. Louis A. Burgess, *Virginia Soldiers of 1776*, vol. 3 (Spartanburg, S.C.: The Reprint Company, 1973), 1278. (Reprinted from a 1929 edition.)

57. Booth, 50–52.

58. Harriette Simpson Arnow, *Flowering of the Cumberland* (New York: Macmillan, 1963), 34–35.

59. Smith, 1811.

60. Bellias, p. 81. Also mentioned in John Richard Alden, *General Charles Lee, Traitor or Patriot* (Baton Rouge: Louisiana State University Press, 1951), 294.

61. Desmond, 191.

62. Booth, 161.

63. Scheer, 161.

64. Marvin Kitman, *George Washington's Expense Account* (New York: Simon & Schuster, 1970), 276.

65. Scheer, 310.

66. Engle, 250.

67. James Thomas Flexner, *Washington, The Indispensable Man* (Boston: Little, Brown, 1974), 134.

68. Eleanor Flexner, *Century of Struggle* (New York: Atheneum, 1973), 119.

69. Mrs. William Lawson Peel, ed., *Historical Collections of the Joseph Habersham Chapter, Daughters of the American Revolution*, vol. 1, (Baltimore: Genealogical Publishing Company, 1967), 33–34.

70. H. R. Wilkins.

CHAPTER 2

1. Col. R. Ernest DuPuy, *The Compact History of the United States Army* (New York: Hawthorne Books, 1963), 48.

2. James Ripley Jacobs, *The Beginning of the U.S. Army, 1783-1812* (Princeton, N.J.: Princeton University Press, 1947), 14.

3. Harriet Simpson Arnow, *Flowering of the Cumberland* (New York: Macmillan, 1963), 30.

4. Jacobs, 16–17.

5. Robert M. Utley, *Frontiersmen in Blue: The United States Army and the Indians, 1848-1865* (New York: Macmillan, 1967), 22.

6. Ralph H. Gabriel, ed., "The Lure of the Frontier," in *The Pageant of America*, vol. 2. (Toronto: U.S. Publishers Association, 1929), 205.

7. Edward M. Coffman, *The Old Army, A Portrait of the American Army in Peacetime, 1784-1898* (New York: Oxford University Press, 1986), 59, 152.

8. Utley, 32.

9. Coffman, 25.

10. Jacobs, 8–9.

11. William H. Guthman, *March to Massacre* (New York: McGraw-Hill, 1970), 228; Jacobs, 89–90.

12. Coffman, 26.

13. Jacobs, 109–11.

14. Sandra L. Myres, *Westering Women and the Frontier Experience* (Albuquerque: University of New Mexico Press, 1982), 50.

15. Allan W. Eckert, *Gateway to Empire* (Boston: Little, Brown, 1983), 533–48.

16. Eckert, 549.

17. Maurice Melton, "War Trail of the Red Sticks," *American History* 10, no. 10 (February 1976): 37–38.

18. Evan Jones, *Citadel in the Wilderness: The Story of Fort Snelling and the Old Northwest Frontier* (New York: Coward-McCann, 1966), 73–74.

19. Grant Foreman, *Advancing the Frontier* (Norman: University of Oklahoma Press, 1933), 63–66.

20. George Walton, *Sentinel of the Plains: Fort Leavenworth and the American West* (Englewood Cliffs, N.J.: Prentice-Hall, 1973), 90.

21. Walton, 11.

22. Walton, 15.

23. Jones, 40.

24. Information in displays at Casemate Museum, Fort Monroe, Virginia.

25. Lucille M. Kane, ed., *Life in Dakota: The Journal of Philippe Regis de Trobriand* (St. Paul, Minn.: Alvord Memorial Commission, 1951), 52–53.

26. Teresa Viele, *Following the Drum, A Glimpse of Frontier Life* (Austin: Steck-Vaughn, 1968), 106–7. (Originally published in 1858.)

27. Viele, 140.

28. Walton, 88.

29. Oliver Knight, *Life and Manners in the Frontier Army* (Norman: University of Oklahoma Press, 1978), 6.

30. Marian T. Place, *Rifles and War Bonnets* (New York: Ives Washburn, 1968), 18.

31. Foreman, 85.

32. Walton, 88.

33. Walton, 89.

34. Mrs. Orsemus B. Boyd, *Cavalry Life in Tent Field* (Lincoln: University of Nebraska Press, 1982), 190–193. (Originally published New York: J. S. Tait, 1894).

35. Jacobs, 27–28.

36. Coffman, 117.

37. Guthman, 61.

38. Francis Paul Prucha, *Broadax and Bayonet* (Lincoln: University of Nebraska Press, 1953), 201.

39. Jones, 75–79.

40. Jacobs, 143.

41. Jones, 75.

42. Foreman, 65.

43. Ruth Ellen Patton Totten, "The Army Wife's Heritage," *Armor* 82 (November–December, 1973): 40.

44. Philip St. George Cooke, *Scenes and Adventures in the Army or Romance of Military Life*. Philadelphia: Lindsay and Blakiston Publishing, 1857, 40. (Reprinted in *The Far Western Frontier* series, New York: Arnow Press, 1973).

45. Major General James A. Wier, "The Wives' Tales," *AMEDD Spectrum* 1, no. 2 (1974): 35.

46. Coffman, 115.

47. Robert V. Hine and Savoie Lottinville, eds., *Soldier in the West* (Norman: University of Oklahoma Press, 1972), 87.

48. Whitton, 22.

49. Nancy Hamilton, "The Great Western," from *The Women Who Made the West* (New York: Avon Books, 1980), 107–8.

CHAPTER 3

1. John Elting (Col. U.S. Army, Retired), *American Army Life* (New York: Charles Scribner's Sons, 1982), 123.

2. Mary Elizabeth Massey, *Bonnet Brigades* (New York: Knopf, 1966), 68.

3. Francis Butler Simkins and James W. Patton, *The Women of the Confederacy* (Richmond: Garrett and Massie, 1936), 213.

4. Bell Irvin Wiley, *The Life of Billy Yank* (Garden City, N.Y.: Doubleday, 1952), 257.

5. Simkins, 116.

6. Henry Steele Commager, *The Blue and the Grey* (New York: Fairfax Press, 1982), 743.

7. C. Vann Woodward and Elisabeth Muhlenfeld, *The Private Mary Chesnut, The Unpublished Civil War Diaries* (New York: Oxford University Press, 1984), 85–86.

8. William W. Fowler, *Women on the American Frontier* (Hartford, Conn.: S.S. Scranton, 1878), 423.

9. Frank Moore, *Women of the War* (Hartford, Conn.: S.S. Scranton, 1866), 255.

10. Moore, 260.

11. Agathy Young, *The Women and the Crisis* (New York: McDowell, Obolensky, 1959), 162.

12. Young, 162–63.

13. Young, 122.

14. Young, 122–23.

15. Job Arnold to Frank Moore, February 2, 1866. (In Manuscript Department, Duke University Library, Durham, N.C.)

16. Elting, 118.

17. Massey, 81.

18. Massey, 68.

19. Freeman Cleaves, *Meade of Gettysburg* (Norman: University of Oklahoma Press, 1960), 307.

20. Massey, 71.

21. Alexander Gardner, *Gardner's Photographic Sketchbook of the Civil War* (New York: Dover Publications, 1959), 57. (Unaltered reproduction of the first edition published in 1866.)

22. Woodward, 86.

23. Wiley, 257.

24. Simkins, 72; Massey, 66.

25. Elting, 119.

26. John Y. Simon, ed., *The Papers of Ulysses S. Grant*, vol. 8, April 1–July 6, 1863 (Carbondale: Southern Illinois University, 1979), 332.

27. Elting, 119; Bruce Catton, *Grant Takes Command* (Boston: Little, Brown, 1969), 113.

28. Simon, 155.

29. Massey, 67.

30. Massey, 66.

31. James M. McPherson, *Battle Cry of Freedom, The Civil War Era* (New York: Ballantine Books, 1988), 479–81.

32. Elizabeth S. Mendenhall to Frank Moore, June 3, 1866. (In Manuscript Department, Duke University Library, Durham, N.C.)

33. Mendenhall.

34. Young, 167.

35. Mendenhall.

CHAPTER 4

1. Robert C. Carriker and Eleanor R. Carriker, eds., *An Army Wife on the Frontier* (Salt Lake City: University of Utah Library, 1975), 29–31.

2. Ganoe, 299, 309.

3. Lucile M. Kane, ed., *Military Life in Dakota: The Journal of Philippe Regis de Trobriand* (St. Paul, Minn.: Alvord Memorial Commission, 1951), 52–53.

4. Sandra Myres, ed., *Cavalry Wife, The Diary of Eveline M. Alexander* (College Station: Texas A & M University Press, 1977), 34.

5. Myres, 37–38.

6. D. Clayton James, *The Years of MacArthur*, vol. 1, 1880-1941 (New York: Houghton Mifflin, 1970), 24–25.

7. James, 50–51.

8. Frances M. A. Roe, *Army Letters from an Officer's Wife* (Lincoln: University of Nebraska Press, 1981), 207. (Originally published New York: D. Appleton, 1909.)

9. Oliver Knight, *Life and Manners in the Frontier Army* (Norman: University of Oklahoma Press, 1978), 3–4.

10. *The Army and Navy Journal*, 16 (June 15, 1878): 721.

11. Irvin Bell Wiley, *The Life of Billy Yank* (Garden City, N.Y.: Doubleday, 1952), 52.

12. Colonel R. Ernest DuPuy, "Pass in Review," *The Army Combat Forces Journal*, 5 (October 1954): 31.

13. Patricia Y. Stallard, *Glittering Misery* (San Rafael, Calif.: Presidio Press; Fort Collins, Colo.: The Old Army Press, 1978), 29.

14. Elizabeth Bacon Custer, *Boots and Saddles* (New York: Harper & Bros., 1885), 103.

15. James, 52.

16. Elizabeth Bacon Custer, *Following the Guidon* (Norman: University of Oklahoma Press, 1966), 2; Dee Brown, *The Gentle Tamers, Women of the Old Wild West* (Lincoln: University of Nebraska Press, 1958), 47.

17. Custer, *Following the Guidon,* 252–53.

18. Roe, 67.

19. Roe, 69.

20. Captain W. S. Nye, *Carbine and Lance: The Story of Old Fort Sill* (Norman: University of Oklahoma Press, 1937), 360.

21. Place, 18–20.

22. Nye, 361.

23. Stallard, 54–57.

24. Assistant Surgeon S. R. Kean, Fort Robinson, Nebraska, letter to the Medical Director, Department of State, Omaha, Nebraska, December 20, 1889 (Archives of Fort Robinson, Nebraska).

25. Captain and Assistant Surgeon George W. Adair, "Enumeration of Women and Children at Fort Robinson, Nebraska, Arranged by Habituation," July 24, 1891 (Archives of Fort Robinson, Nebraska).

26. Foreman, 85.

27. Roe, 223.

28. John M. Sibbald, "Army Women of the West," *The Retired Officer*, 23, no. 3 (April 1967): 17.

29. Stallard, 54–57.

30. Custer, *Boots and Saddles*, 254.

31. Emily Fitzgerald McCorkle, *An Army Doctor's Wife on the Frontier*, Abe Laufe, ed. (Pittsburgh: University of Pittsburgh Press, 1962), 195–96.

32. Margaret Irvin Carrington, *Absaraka* (Lincoln: University of Nebraska Press, 1983), 92. (Originally published Philadelphia: J. B. Lippincott, 1868.)

33. Thomas R. Buecker, ed., "Letters from a Post Surgeon's Wife, The Fort Washakie Correspondence of Caroline Frey Winne, May 1879-May 1880," Charles W. Taylor Collection, U.S. Military Academy Museum, 45–46.

34. From the unpublished memoirs of General Eli Helmick.

35. Carrington, 175.

36. Robert C. Athearn, *Forts of the Upper Missouri* (Englewood Cliffs, N.J.: Prentice-Hall, 1967), 47.

37. Coffman, 315.

38. Custer, *Following the Guidon*, 227.

39. Roe, 75.

40. Roe, 76–77.

41. Carrington, 96–129.

42. Totten, 42.

43. Totten, 42.

44. McCorkle, 301–2

45. Brown, 51–58.

46. Myres, 178–79.

47. Custer, *Boots and Saddles*, 83–88.

48. From the unpublished memoirs of General Eli Helmick.

49. Boyd, 199.

50. Roe, 25–27.

51. Myres, 63–78.

52. Knight, 3.

53. Nye, 361.

54. Coffman, 311.

55. Knight, 42–43.

56. General James Parker, *The Old Army, Memories 1872-1918* (Philadelphia: Dorrance & Company, 1929), 117–23.

57. Knight, 41–42.
58. Knight, 42.
59. Knight, 42.
60. Custer, *Boots and Saddles*, 119.
61. Kean.
62. Kean.

CHAPTER 5

1. All material regarding Elizabeth Helmick is from the memoirs of her husband, General Eli Helmick, or personal communication with her daughter, Mrs. Florence Helmick Pinkerton, February 1986.

2. Emily Fitzgerald McCorkle, *An Army Doctor's Wife on the Frontier*, Abe Laufe, ed. (Pittsburgh: University of Pittsburgh Press, 1962), 44–47.

3. Barendina G. Chambers, Sketches of her childhood in Alaska (5th sketch) *The Kentuckian Citizen* (1959). (From the Carlyle Barracks, Pennsylvania.)

4. I. B. Holley, Jr., *General John M. Palmer, Citizen Soldiers and the Army of a Democracy* (Westport, Conn.: Greenwood Press, 1982), 99–100.

5. General James Parker, *The Old Army, Memories 1872–1918* (Philadelphia: Dorrance & Company, 1929), 400.

6. Allan R. Millett, *The General, Robert L. Bullard and Officership in the United States Army, 1881–1925* (Westport, Conn.: Greenwood Press, 1975), 196–97.

7. Holley, 169, 172.

8. Holley, 169–72.

9. David Howard Bain, *Sitting in Darkness, Americans in the Philippines* (Boston: Houghton Mifflin, 1984), 78.

10. Holley, 172.

11. Colonel R. Ernest DuPuy, *The Army Combat Forces Journal*, 5 (October 1954): 37.

12. All material regarding Bessie Edwards from a letter dated August 26, 1959, Schofield Barracks, Hawaii.

13. DuPuy, 34–35.

14. Patricia Alvarez, *A History of Schofield Barracks Military Reservation* (Department of the Army, U.S. Army Engineer Division Pacific Ocean, Fort Shafter, Hawaii, March 1982), 30.

15. All material regarding Carita Rodby from unpublished interview by Ann Joesting, January 28, 1971. Used with permission of Dick Rodby, son.

16. Alvarez, 28.

CHAPTER 6

1. All material regarding Marie Pope Lee from personal communication, November 1986.

2. *The American Heritage History of World War I* (New York: American Heritage Publishing Company, 1964), narrative by S. L. A. Marshall.

3. All material regarding Phyllis Weisburgh Levantine from personal communication, November 8, 1986.

4. Martin Blumenson, *The Patton Papers, 1885-1940* (Boston: Houghton Mifflin, 1972), 405–6.

5. Blumenson, 405.

6. All material regarding Mary Leontine Bartow from personal communication, January 1986.

7. E. B. Potter, *Bull Halsey* (Annapolis, Md.: Naval Institute Press, 1984), 123–24.

8. William Addleman Ganoe, *The History of the United States Army*, rev. ed., (Ashton, Md.: Eric Lundberg, 1964), 478.

9. Ganoe, 479–82.

10. Ganoe, 482–83.

11. Ganoe, 484.

12. Robert K. Griffith, Jr., *Men Wanted for the U.S. Army* (Westport, Conn.: Greenwood Press, 1982), 204.

13. Griffith, 75.

14. Griffith, 155.

15. Griffith, 155.

16. Griffith, 156.

17. Griffith, 156.

18. Griffith, 156–57.

19. Griffith, 155.

20. John Elting (Col. U.S. Army, Retired), *American Army Life* (New York: Charles Scribner's Sons, 1982), 227.

21. Griffith, 203.

22. Griffith, 204.

23. Colonel R. Ernest DuPuy, *The Army Combat Forces Journal*, 5 (October 1954): 34–35.

24. Lowell Thomas and Edward Jablonski, *Doolittle, A Biography* (New York: Doubleday, 1976), 69.

25. Omar N. Bradley and Clay Blair, *A General's Life* (Simon & Schuster, 1955), 50, 55.

26. Leonard Mosley, *Hero for Our Times*, (New York: Hearst Books, 1982), 91.

27. All material regarding Eva Moore Higgins from personal communication, June 22, 1989.

28. Dupuy, 39.

29. Potter, 123–24.

30. All material regarding Harriet Marshall Olson from personal communication, June 3, 1990.

CHAPTER 7

1. All material regarding Lucille Giordano Ritzus from personal communication, May 1990.

2. John Elting (Col. U.S. Army, Retired), *American Army Life* (New York: Charles Scribner's Sons, 1982), 247.

3. *Yank*, 1, no. 4 (July 8, 1942): 4.

4. All material regarding Leontine Thodarson Briggs from personal communication, January 8, 1986.

5. Phyllis Thompson Wright, *A Navy Wife's Log* (Washington, D.C.: Andromeda Books, 1979), 66, 71.

6. All material regarding Elva J. Maughan from personal communication, June 1990.

7. "The Missus Gets $50—Regardless," *Yank*, 1, no. 6 (July 22, 1942): 3.

8. John D. Millett, *United States Army in World War II, The Organization and Role of the Army Service Forces* (Washington, D.C.: Office of the Chief of Military History, Department of the Army, 1954), 261.

9. Elting, 256.

10. "Gals behind the Guns," *Yank*, 1, no. 14 (September 16, 1942): 9.

11. All material regarding Nadine Ruspini Morton from personal communication, April 1990.

12. All material regarding Myrthel Strand Fuller from personal communication, May 25, 1990.

13. All material regarding Placido Lucero Sorrell from personal communication, February 7, 1990.

14. All material regarding Clarice Matthewson Corboy from personal communication, March 1986.

15. Elting, 256–57.

16. Bernadine V. Lee, "Army Wife in Tokyo," *The Army Information Digest* 1 (December 1, 1946): 15–16.

17. Lee, 17–18.

18. Lee, 18–22.

19. William C. Chase, *Front Line General: The Commands of Major General William C. Chase* (Houston: Pacesetter Press, 1975), 154.

20. All material regarding Jeanne D'Arcy Vaughn from personal communication, February 22, 1986.

21. Eva Ekvall, "China Trek," *Army Information Digest* 3 (August 3, 1948): 49–51.

22. All material regarding Caroline Truitt Giamario from personal communication, June 12, 1986.

23. Lieutenant Irene S. Taylor, "Army Wives Afloat," *The Army Information Digest*, 2 (May 2, 1947): 15–17.

24. Taylor, 21–22.

25. All information regarding Herta Lund Madsen from personal communication, June 5, 1990.

CHAPTER 8

1. Rockford Institute Center on the Family in America, "You're in the Army Now: The Troubled State of the Military Family," *The Family in America* 3, no. 11, (November 1989): 2–3.

2. Nancy L. Goldman and David R. Segal, eds., "Trends in Family Patterns of U.S. Military Personnel During the 20th Century," in *The Social Psychology of Military Service* (Beverly Hills: Sage Publications, 1976), 120.

3. Morris Janowitz, *The Professional Soldier* (Glencoe, Ill.: Free Press, 1961), 182.

4. Janowitz, 181–82.

5. Janowitz, 15.

6. *The Report of the President's Commission on an All-Volunteer Armed Force* (London: Collier Books/Macmillan, 1970), 122.

7. Rockford Institute, 4.

8. Sara A. Levitan, and Karen Cleary Alderman, *Warriors at Work* (Beverly Hills: Sage Publications, 1977), 55.

9. All material regarding Julia Litvack Vean from personal communication, June 5, 1990.

10. All material regarding Ginger Sullivan from personal communication, January 21, 1986.

11. All material regarding Marie Long Smith from personal communication, June 24, 1989.

12. Rockford Institute, 3.

13. Janowitz, 206.

14. Rockford Institute, 3.

15. Nancy Shea, *The Army Wife* (New York: Harper & Bros., 1954), 107.

16. Helen Todd Westpheling, *Army Lady Today* (Charlotte, N.C.: Heritage House, 1959), 7.

17. Nancy Shea, *The Army Wife*, revised by Anna Perle Smith (New York: Harper & Row, 1966), 7–8.

18. Mary Preston Gross, *Mrs. NCO* (Chuluota, Fla.: Beau Lac Publishers, 1969), 10.

19. Shea, 1966, 9.

20. All material regarding Joan Brennan McDavid from personal communication, September 11, 1990.

21. All material regarding Julie Farnsworth from personal communication, December 18, 1986.

22. All material regarding Judith Smith Lott from personal communication, September 12, 1990.

23. All material regarding Faith Louise Dix from personal communication, October 21, 1986.

24. All material regarding Mildred Schwab Martinez from personal communication, June 5, 1990.

25. Aphrodite Matsakis, *Vietnam Wives*. Woodbine House, 1988. xiii.

CHAPTER 9

1. Reuben Hill, *Families Under Stress: Adjustment to the Crises of War, Separation and Reunion* (Westport, Conn.: Greenwood Press: 1949), 7.

2. Hill, 9.

3. Hill, 82.

4. Hill, 82.

5. Richard A. Isay, "The Submariners' Wives Syndrome," *Psychiatric Quarterly*, 42, no. 4 (October 1968): 647.

6. Chester A. Pearlman, "Separation Reactions of Married Women." *American Journal of Psychiatry*, 126, no. 7 (January 1970): 946.

7. Pearlman, 946–47.

8. Robert W. Bermudes, "A Ministry to the Repeatedly Grief Stricken," *Journal of Pastoral Care*, 27 (1973): 218.

9. Alice Ivey Snyder, "Sea and Shore Rotation: The Family and Separation," Office of Naval Research, Department of the Navy (October 1, 1977), 125.

10. Grant Willis, "Study Links Officer Retention, Spouse Jobs," *Air Force Times*, April 18, 1989, 14.

11. Mario R. Schwabe and Florence W. Kaslow, "Violence in the Military Family, Florence W. Kaslow and Richard I. Ridenour, eds., *The Military Family, Dynamics and Treatment* (New York: The Guilford Press, 1984), 129–30.

12. Edna J. Hunter, *A Review of Military Family Literature* (New York: Praeger, 1982), 10.

13. All information regarding Harriet Weissman from personal communication, January 17, 1987.

14. All information regarding Mary Beth Mills from personal communication, February 10, 1986.

15. All material regarding Sandra Paige from personal communication, February 19, 1987.

16. All material regarding Roberta Junge from personal communication, June 11, 1986.

17. All material regarding Jean Woods from personal communication, August 12, 1986.

BIBLIOGRAPHY

Adair, George W. "Enumeration of Women and Children at Fort Robinson, Nebraska, Arranged by Habituation." July 24, 1891. Archives at Fort Robinson, Nebraska.

Addleman, William C. *A History of the U.S. Army in Hawaii, 1849-1939.* Division Headquarters Detachment, Hawaiian Division, Schofield Barracks, Territory of Hawaii.

Alden, John Richard. *General Charles Lee, Traitor or Patriot.* Baton Rouge: Louisiana State University Press, 1951.

Alvarez, Patricia. "A History of Schofield Barracks Military Reservation." Department of the Army, U.S. Army Engineer Division Pacific Ocean, Fort Shafter, Hawaii (March 1982).

The American Heritage History of World War I. New York: American Heritage Publishing Company, 1964 (narrative by S. L. A. Marshall).

American History, February 1976.

The Army and Navy Journal, June 15, 1878.

The Army Family. White Paper 1983 by the Chief of Staff, U.S. Army, 15 August 1983.

Arnold, Job. Letter to Frank Moore, February 2, 1866. Manuscript Department, Duke University Library, Durham, N.C.

Arnow, Harriette Simpson. *Flowering of the Cumberland.* (New York: Macmillan, 1963.

Athearn, Robert C. *Forts of the Upper Mississippi.* Englewood Cliffs, N.J.: Prentice-Hall, 1967.

Bellairs, Edgar G. *As It Is in the Philippines.* New York: Lewis Scribner & Company, 1902.

Bellias, Georth Athan, ed. *George Washington's Generals.* (New York: William Morrow, 1964.

Bermudes, Robert W. "A Ministry to the Repeatedly Grief Stricken." *Journal of Pastoral Care* 27 (1973): 218-28.

Billings, John D. *Hard Tack and Coffee or The Unwritten Story of Army Life*. Williamstown, Mass.: Corner House Publishers, 1973. First published in 1887.

Blumenson, Martin. *The Patton Papers, 1885-1940*. Boston: Houghton Mifflin, 1972.

Booth, Sally Smith. *The Women of '76*. New York: Hastings House, 1973.

Boyd, Mrs. Orsemus. *Cavalry Life in Tent and Field*. Lincoln: University of Nebraska Press, 1982. Originally published New York: J. S. Tait, 1894.

Bradley, Omar N. and Clay Blair. *A General's Life*. New York: Simon & Schuster, 1955.

Brown, Dee. *The Gentle Tamers: Women of the Old Wild West*. Lincoln: University of Nebraska Press, 1958.

Bryant, Ruth. "An Army Wife in Manila." *The Army Information Digest* (February 1948): 35–42.

Buecker, Thomas R., ed. "Letters from a Post Surgeon's Wife." The Fort Washakie correspondence of Caroline Frey Winne, May 1879-May 1880. Charles W. Taylor Collection, U.S. Military Academy.

Burgess, Louis A. *Virginia Soldiers of 1776*, vol. 3. Spartanburg, S.C.: The Reprint Company, 1973. Reprinted from a 1929 edition.

Carriker, Robert C. and Eleanor R. Carriker, eds. *An Army Wife on the Frontier*. Salt Lake City: University of Utah Library, 1975.

Carrington, Margaret Irvin. *Absaraka*. Lincoln: University of Nebraska Press, 1983. Originally published Philadelphia: J. B. Lippincott, 1868.

Chase, William C. *Front Line General: The Commands of Major General William C. Chase*. Houston: Pacesetter Press, 1975.

Cleaves, Freeman. *Meade of Gettysburg*. Norman: University of Oklahoma Press, 1960.

Coffman, Edward M. *The Old Army: A Portrait of the American Army in Peacetime, 1784-1898*. New York: Oxford University Press, 1986.

Commager, Henry Steele. *The Blue and the Grey*. New York: Fairfax Press, 1982.

Cooke, Philip St. George. *Scenes and Adventures in the Army or Romance of Military Life*. Philadelphia: Lindsay and Blakiston Publishing, 1857. Reprinted in *The Far Western Frontier* series, New York: Arnow Press, 1973.

Custer, Elizabeth Bacon. *Boots and Saddles*. New York: Harper & Brothers, 1885.

_____. *Following the Guidon*. (Norman: University of Oklahoma Press, 1966.

Davis, Burke. *George Washington and the American Revolution*. New York: Random House, 1975.

DePauw, Linda Grant. *Founding Mothers*. (Boston: Houghton Mifflin, 1975.

Desmond, Alice Curtis. *Martha Washington: Our First Lady*. New York: Dodd Mead, 1976.

Donovan, Frank. *The George Washington Papers*. New York: Dodd Mead, 1964.

DuPuy, R. Ernest. "Pass in Review." *The Army Combat Forces Journal* 5 (October 1954).: 27–39.

_____. *The Compact History of the United States Army*. New York: Hawthorne Books, 1963.

Eckert, Allan W. *Gateway to Empire*. Boston: Little, Brown, 1983.

Edwards, Bessie. Unpublished letters to the Commanding Officer, Schofield Barracks, Oahu, Hawaii, dated August 26, 1957. Courtesy of the Public Affairs Officer, Fort Shafter, Hawaii.

Ekvall, Eva. "China Trek." *The Army Information Digest* 3 (August 1948): 49–52.

Ellet, Elizabeth F. *The Women of the American Revolution*, vol. 2, 4th ed. New York: Haskell House, 1969.

Elting, John. *American Army Life*. New York: Charles Scribner's Sons, 1982.

Engle, Paul. *Women in the American Revolution*. Chicago: Follett Publishing Company, 1976.

Evans, Elizabeth. *Weathering the Storm*. New York: Charles Scribner & Sons, 1975.

Fleming, Thomas. *1776, Year of Illusion*. New York: W. W. Norton, 1975.

Flexner, Eleanor. *Century of Struggle*. New York: Atheneum, 1973.

Flexner, James Thomas. *Washington, The Indispensable Man*. Boston: Little, Brown, 1974.

Foreman, Grant. *Advancing the Frontier*. Norman: University of Oklahoma Press, 1933.

Fowler, William W. *Women on the American Frontier*. Hartford, Conn.: S. S. Scranton, 1878.

Freeman, Cleaves. *Meade of Gettysburg*. Norman: University of Oklahoma Press, 1960.

Gabriel, Ralph H., ed. "The Lure of the Frontier," in *The Pageant of America*, vol. 2. Toronto: U.S. Publishers Association, 1929.

Ganoe, William Addleman. *The History of the United States Army*. New York: D. Appleton-Century, 1942.

_____. *The History of the United States Army*, rev. ed. Ashton, Md.: Eric Lundberg, 1964.

Gardner, Alexander. *Gardner's Photographic Sketchbook of the Civil War*. New York: Dover Publications, 1959. Unaltered reproduction of the first edition published in 1866.

Goldman, Nancy L. and David R. Segal. The Social Psychology of Military Service, vol. 6. Beverly Hills: Sage Publications, 1976.

Griffith, Robert K., Jr. *Men Wanted for the U.S. Army.* Westport, Conn.: Greenwood Press, 1982.

Gross, Mary Preston. *Mrs. NCO.* Chuluota, Fla.: Beau Lac Publishers, 1969.

Guthman, William H. *March to Massacre.* New York: McGraw-Hill, 1970.

Hamilton, Nancy. "The Great Western," from *The Women Who Made the West.* Avon Books, 1980.

Harkness, David James. "Heroines of the American Revolution." *University of Tennessee Newsletter* 40, no. 1 (February 1961): 1-19.

Helmick, Eli. Unpublished memoirs with permission of Margaret M. Woods.

Helmick, Elizabeth. Unpublished diary with permission of Margaret M. Woods.

Hill, Reuben. *Families Under Stress, Adjustment to the Crises of War, Separation and Reunion.* Westport, Conn.: Greenwood Press, 1949.

Hine, Robert V. and Savoie Lottinville, eds. *Soldier in the West.* Norman: University of Oklahoma Press, 1972.

Hunter, Edna J. *A Review of Military Family Literature.* New York: Praeger, 1982.

Isay, Richard A. "The Submariners' Wives Syndrome." *Psychiatric Quarterly* 42, no. 4 (October 1968): 647-52.

Jacobs, James Ripley. *The Beginning of the U.S. Army, 1783-1812.* Princeton: Princeton University Press, 1947.

James, D. Clayton. *The Years of MacArthur,* volume 1, 1880-1941. Boston: Houghton Mifflin, 1970.

Janowitz, Morris. *The Professional Soldier.* Glencoe, Ill.: The Free Press, 1961.

Johnson, Virginia Weisel. *Lady in Arms.* Boston: Houghton Mifflin, 1967.

Jones, Evan. *Citadel in the Wilderness: The Story of Fort Snelling and the Old Northwest Frontier.* New York: Coward-McCann, 1966.

Kane, Lucille M., ed. *Life in Dakota: The Journal of Philippe Regis de Trobriand.* St. Paul, Minn.: Alvord Memorial Commission, 1951.

Kean, S. R. Letter to the Medical Director, Department of State, Omaha, Nebraska, December 20, 1889. Archives at Fort Robinson, Nebraska.

Kitman, Marvin. *George Washington's Expense Account.* New York: Simon & Schuster, 1970.

Knight, Oliver. *Life and Manners in the Frontier Army.* Norman: University of Oklahoma Press, 1978.

Laffin, John. *Women in Battle.* London: Abelard-Schuman, 1967.

Lee, Bernadine. "Army Wife in Tokyo." *The Army Information Digest.* 1 (December 1946): 14-22.

Little, Roger W., ed. *Handbook of Military Institutions.* Beverly Hills: Sage Publications, 1971.

Logan, Mrs. John A. *The Part Taken by Women in American History*. Wilmington: Perry-Nalle, 1912.

Mariotta, Franklin D., ed. *The Changing World of the American Military*. Boulder: Westview Press, 1978.

Martin, James A. and Jeanette R. Ickovics. "Challenges of Military Life: The Importance of a Partnership Between the Army and Its Families." *Military Family 6, no. 6 (November-December 1986): 3-5*.

Massey, Mary Elizabeth. *Bonnet Brigades*. New York: Knopf, 1966.

Mattes, Merrill J. *Indians, Infants and Infantry*. Denver: Old West Publishing Company, 1960.

Maus, Louis Mervin. *An Army Officer on Leave in Japan*. Chicago: McClurg and Company, 1911.

McCorkle, Emily Fitzgerald. *An Army Doctor's Wife on the Frontier*, Abe Laufe, ed. Pittsburgh: University of Pittsburgh Press, 1962.

McGuire, Judith W. *Diary of a Southern Refugee During the War*. Richmond: 1889.

McPherson, James M. *Battle Cry of Freedom: The Civil War Era*. New York: Ballantine Books, 1988.

Mendenhall, Elizabeth S. Letter to Frank Moore, June 3, 1866. Manuscript Department, Duke University Library, Durham, N.C.

Millet, John D. *United States Army in World War II, The Organization and Role of the Army Service Forces*. Washington, D.C.: Office of the Chief of Military History, Department of the Army, 1954.

Montross, Lynn. *The Story of the Continental Army, 1775-1783*. New York: Barnes & Noble, 1952.

Moore, Frank. *Women of the War*. Hartford, Conn.: S.S. Scranton, 1866.

Mosley, Leonard. *Hero for Our Times*. New York: Hearst Books, 1982.

Myres, Sandra L. *Westering Women and the Frontier Experience*. Albuquerque: University of New Mexico Press, 1982.

Nye, W. S. *Carbine and Lance: The Story of Old Fort Sill*. Norman: University of Oklahoma Press, 1937.

Parker, James. *The Old Army, Memories 1872-1918*. Philadelphia: Dorrance & Company, 1929.

Pearlman, Chester A. "Separation Reactions of Married Women." *American Journal of Psychiatry* 126, no. 7 (January 1970): 946-500.

Peel, Mrs. William Lawson, ed. *Historical Collections of the Joseph Habersham Chapter, Daughters of the American Revolution*, vol. 2. Baltimore: Genealogical Publishing Company, 1967.

Place, Marian T. *Rifles and War Bonnets*. New York: Ives Washburn, 1968.

Potter, E. B. *Bull Halsey*. Annapolis: Naval Institute Press, 1984.

Prucha, Francis Paul. *Broadax and Bayonet*. Lincoln: University of Nebraska Press, 1953.

Rockford Institute Center on the Family in America. " 'You're in the Army Now': The Troubled State of the Military Family." *The Family in America* 3, no. 11 (November 1989): 2–3.

Roe, Frances M. A., *Army Letters from an Officer's Wife.* Lincoln: University of Nebraska Press, 1987.

Sarkesian, Sam C. *The Professional Army Officer in a Changing Society.* Chicago: Nelson-Hall, 1975.

Scheer, George F. and Hugh F. Rankin. *Rebels and Redcoats.* New York: World Publishing, 1957.

Schwabe, Mario R. and Florence W. Kaslow. "Violence in the Military Family," in Florence W. Kaslow and Richard I. Ridenour, eds. *The Military Family, Dynamics and Treatment.* New York: Guilford Press, 1984.

Shea, Nancy. *The Army Wife.* New York: Harper & Bros., 1954.

Shea, Nancy, revised by Anna Perle Smith. *The Army Wife.* New York: Harper & Row, 1966.

Sibbald, John R. "Army Women of the West, Campfollowers All." *The Retired Officer* 23, no. 3 (April 1967): 16–21.

Simkins, Francis Butler and James W. Patton. *The Women of the Confederacy.* Richmond: Garrett and Massie, 1936.

Simon, John Y., ed. *The Papers of Ulysses S. Grant,* vol. 8, April 1–July 6, 1863. Carbondale: Southern Illinois University Press, 1979.

Smith, Page. *A New Age Now Begins,* vol. 2. New York: McGraw-Hill, 1976.

Snyder, Alice Ivey. "Sea and Shore Rotation: The Family and Separation." Office of Naval Research, Department of the Navy (October 1, 1977).

Stallard, Patricia Y. *Glittering Misery.* San Rafael, Calif.: Presidio Press; Fort Collins, Colo.: The Old Army Press, 1978.

Stratton, Joanna L. *Pioneer Women, Voices from the Kansas Frontier.* New York: Simon & Schuster, 1981.

Taylor, Irene S. "Army Wives Afloat." *The Army Information Digest* 22 (May 1947): 15–22.

Thomas, Lowell and Edward Jablonski. *Doolittle, A Biography.* New York: Doubleday, 1976.

Totten, Ruth Ellen Patton. "The Army Wife's Heritage." *Armour,* 82, no. 6 (November-December 1973): 39–44.

Utley, Beverly. "Women of the Revolution. In *The Uncommon Soldier of the Revolution.* Philadelphia: Eastern Acorn Press, 1986. With permission of the original Publisher, Historical Times, Harrisburg.

Utley, Robert M. *Frontiersmen in Blue: The United States Army and the Indians, 1848-1865.* New York: Macmillan, 1967.

Viele, Teresa. *Following the Drum, A Glimpse of Frontier Life.* Austin: Steck-Vaughn, 1968. Originally published in 1858.

Walton, George. *Sentinel of the Plains: Fort Leavenworth and the American West.* Englewood Cliffs, N.J.: Prentice-Hall, 1973.

Ward, Christopher. *The War of the Revolution,* vol. 2, John Richard Alden, ed. New York: Macmillan, 1952.

Ward, Just. *Military Men.* New York: Knopf, 1970.

Westpheling, Helen Todd. *Army Lady Today.* Charlotte, N.C.: Heritage House, 1959.

Wharton, Anne Hollingsworth. *Colonial Days and Dames.* Philadelphia: J. B. Lippincott, 1895.

Whitton, Mary Ormsbee. *These Were the Women, USA 1776-1860.* New York: Random House, 1954.

Wier, James A. "The Wives' Tales." *AMEDD Spectrum* 1, no. 2 (1974): 31–39.

Wiley, Irvin Bell. *The Life of Billy Yank.* Garden City, N.Y.: Doubleday, 1952.

Wilkins, H. R. Spartanburg, S.C., 1963.

Willis, Grant. "Study Links Officer Retention, Spouse Jobs." *Air Force Times,* April 18, 1989.

Woodward, C. Vann and Elisabeth Muhlenfeld. *The Private Mary Chesnut: The Unpublished Civil War Diaries.* New York: Oxford University Press, 1984.

Wright, Phyllis Thompson. *A Navy Wife's Log.* Washington, D.C.: Andromeda Books, 1979.

Yank. 1, no. 4 (July 8, 1942): 4.

_____. "The Missus Gets $50—Regardless." 1, no. 6 (July 22, 1942): 3.

_____. "Gals behind the Guns." 1, no. 14 (September 16, 1942): 8–9.

Young, Agatha. *The Women and the Crisis.* New York: McDowell, Obolensky, 1959.

PERSONAL COMMUNICATIONS

Authors gathered all materials through personal interviews, unless noted otherwise.

Bartow, Mary Leontine, July 1986.

Briggs, Leontine Thodarson, January 8, 1986.

Corboy, Clarice Matthewson, March 1986.

Dix, Faith Louise, October 21, 1986.

Farnsworth, Julie, December 18, 1986.

Fuller, Myrthel Strand, May 25, 1990.

Giamario, Caroline Truitt, June 12, 1986.

Higgins, Eva Moore, June 22, 1989.

Junge, Roberta, June 11, 1986.
Lee, Marie Pope, November 1986.
Levantine, Phyllis Weisburgh, November 8, 1986.
Lott, Judith Smith, September 12, 1990.
Madsen, Herta Lund, June 5, 1990.
Martinez, Mildred Schwab, June 5, 1990.
Maughan, Elva J., June 1990.
McDavid, Joan Brennan, September 11, 1990.
Mills, Mary Beth, February 10, 1986.
Morton, Nadine Ruspini, April 1990.
Olson, Harriet Marshall, June 3, 1990. Letter.
Paige, Sandy, February 19, 1987.
Pinkerton, Florence Helmick, February 1986, and unpublished diaries.
Ritzus, Lucille Giordano, May 1990.
Smith, Marie Long, June 24, 1989.
Sorrell, Placido Lucero, February 7, 1990.
Sullivan, Ginger, January 21, 1986.
Vaughn, Jeanne D'Arcy, February 22, 1986.
Vean, Julia Litvack, June 5, 1990.
Weissman, Harriet, January 17, 1987.
Woods, Jean, August 12, 1986.

INDEX

ABOUT THE AUTHORS

BETTY SOWERS ALT has a B.A. degree in sociology from Colorado College and an M.A. in history from Northeast Missouri State University. While following her husband, recently retired Air Force Colonel Bill Alt, around the world, she has lectured on womens' studies issues and taught at the college level. Presently, she is an instructor in the sociology department at the University of Colorado at Colorado Springs.

BONNIE DOMROSE STONE earned her dgree in journalism from Marquette University College of Journalism. She is a former award-winning newspaper reporter and editor for family sections of both daily and weekly newspapers in cities where her husband, retired Senior Chief Leighton F. Stone, was stationed. She freelanced as a magazine article writer before co-authoring her first history book, *Aloha Cowboy*. At present she is an instructor for the University of California at Los Angeles (UCLA) Writers' Extension.